AS THEY HEAD FOR THE
CHECKERS

Fantastic Finishes, Memorable Milestones and Heroes Remembered from the World of Racing

by

KATHY PERSINGER

SPORTS
PUBLISHING
L.L.C.

www.SportsPublishingLLC.com

AS THEY HEAD FOR THE
CHECKERS

Coordinating Editor: Lynnette A. Bogard

Senior Graphic Designer & Project Manager: Kenneth J. O'Brien

Publisher: Peter L. Bannon

Senior Managing Editors: Joseph J. Bannon, Jr. and Susan M. Moyer

Art Director: K. Jeffrey Higgerson

Copy Editor: Cynthia L. McNew

www.SportsPublishingLLC.com

ISBN# 1-58261-590-X

Credits

Photo

FRONT COVER PHOTOS:

From left to right:
AP/Wide World Photo – Dave Kennedy
AP Wide World Photo
AP Wide World Photo – John Bazemore
AP Wide World Photo

BACK COVER PHOTO:

AP Wide World Photo – Mark Foley

Bobby Allison personal collection: 25, 78, 81
Buddy Baker personal collection: 58, 59
David T. Foster, III: 137

AP/WideWorld Photos:
12, 20, 56, 57, 62, 65, 79, 87, 100, 101, 102, 103, 104, 107
Dale Atkins: 97
John Bazemore: 82
Brich: 60
Bob Brodbeck: 133
Rusty Burroughs: 96
Chuck Burton: 47, 61, 63 (top), 84, 88, 93, 94, 95, 99, 122, 146, 147, 152
TC: 13
Barry Carr: 36

Stephen J. Carrera: 140, 142, 143, 153
Mary Ann Chastain: 83, 112
Phil Coale: 70, 90
Curtis Compton: 115
Jim Cole: 45
Pat Crowe, II: 132, 145, 149
Alan Diaz: 109
Ric Feld: 16, 17, 18, 19, 44, 131, 141
Mike Fiala: 86 (bottom)
Mark Foley: 21, 52
Chris Gardner: 150, 151
David Graham: 4, 114
Tony Gutierrez: 125
Russ Hamilton: 24
Mark Humphrey: 10, 11, 56
Eric Jamison: 157
James P. Kerlin: 105
Lou Krasky: 49
Don Larson: 85
Jon Pierre Lasseigne: 37
Will Lester: 158, 159
Chuck Luzier: 68, 69, 71
Alan Marler: 63 (bottom)
Mike McCain: 148
Chris O'Meara: 43, 86 (top), 92
Wade Payne: 134, 135
Terry Renna: 38
Frank Russell: 116
PKS: 15

Paul Sancya: 144
Reed Saxon: 22, 66
Bill Sikes: 91
Steve Simoneau: 53
Joe Skipper: 72
John S. Stewart: 110
Tom Strattman: 138, 139
Greg Suvino: 127
Mark J. Terrill: 154, 155
Chuck Zoeller: 89

The Charlotte Observer:
Gary O'Brien: 29, 30, 31

Getty Images:
Jon Ferry: 111, 123
Jeff Gross: 28
Jim Gund: 106, 108
Bill Hall: 27, 113
Craig Jones: 48
Robert Laberge: 118, 121, 136
Donald Miralle: 73
Mike Powell: 74, 75, 76, 77
Jamie Squire: 6, 7, 124, 128, 129
Chris Stanford: 50, 51, 54
Steve Swope: 26, 32, 33, 34, 35
David Taylor: 40, 41

Audio

MARK GARROW: With a Dad who was a flagman and a mom who scored races at their local short track, Mark Garrow has been around racing just about his whole life. He's spent the last two decades as radio and television broadcaster following NASCAR's top circuit.

Currently, Mark serves as co-anchor for the race broadcasts on The Performance Racing Network (PRN). He also hosts PRN's Garage Pass, a daily show heard on over 450 radio stations nationwide and NASCAR.com, providing fans with the latest NASCAR news. Considered one of the hardest working journalists in motorsports today, Mark has earned numerous awards for his work. He resides in Midway, NC, with his wife, Lynne, and their children, Breanna and Marissa.

Acknowledgments

When Joe Bannon Jr. first approached me about doing a book of this magnitude I was instantly enthusiastic but naturally concerned. What if we missed something? What if some of the events that we chose weren't considered by others to be worthy of mention? After pondering this quandary for a bit I decided it didn't matter. Rarely does everyone have the same opinion about anything, and with racing, you can rest assured that it happens even more often. With all of the stirring moments, colorful personalities and tragic mishaps along with the sport's passionate fan base, I hope we were able to capture the essence of where this sport started and where it is going.

We tried our best to make a good book about a great sport. We certainly could not have done that without the help of Kathy Persinger; she has an interesting and extremely informed view of the world of NASCAR. Our grateful thanks to Kathy not only for sharing her expertise, but also for giving us her gifted style of writing.

Thank you also to Mark Garrow, whose time and meticulous attention to detail brought us the best audio available for the accompanying CD.

Thank you to Joe Bannon, Jr., Susan Moyer, Jeff Higgerson, Kenny O'Brien and Erin Linden-Levy, I appreciate all of your help and guidance.

To my husband, David, and children, Autumn, Taylor and Elizabeth, thank you for being patient as I have worked on this book and for being part of that ever-growing fan base.

Lynnette Bogard
Coordinating Editor

Fantastic Finishes 10

Milestones 46

Tributes 98

New Generations 130

FANTASTIC FINISHES

The 1976 Daytona 500: A Slow Roller

Petty vs. Pearson. Pearson vs. Petty. Those two drivers had one of the most intense rivalries in the history of NASCAR.

David Pearson won the Winston Cup championship three times. Richard Petty won it seven times.

Side by side, the numbers favor Petty. But in one of the greatest finishes of all time, in the 1976 Daytona 500, the victory went to Pearson—the only time he ever won the Great American Race.

A guy named Ramo Scott was on the pole, in a Chevrolet. Pearson, in the Wood Brothers No. 21 Mercury, led only 37 laps total, and, with the exception of one lap led by 1976 Winston Cup champion Benny Parsons, Pearson and Petty, in his No. 43 Dodge, owned the last 46 laps of the race.

They swapped positions three times: Pearson led Laps 155-165; Petty led Laps 166-175; Parsons led Lap

176. Pearson led the next 11 laps and Petty the next 12 after that.

Then came the last half-lap.

Pearson drafted past Petty going into Turn 3, then slipped high, and Petty moved underneath him. They sped side by side through Turn 4 but made contact coming out of the corner.

"I got into the wall and came off and hit him," Pearson said later. "That's what started all the spinning, I think."

All the spinning had Petty crashing into the outside wall, then spiraling into the grass a few yards from the finish line. Pearson swirled into the pit entrance, made contact with the car of Joe Frasson, then spun back toward the track. He would claim, later, that his keeping the clutch engaged kept the motor running, and when the smoke cleared, Pearson's car moseyed across the finish line. One witness said the Mercury must have been going all of five mph.

Petty's crew attempted to push his Dodge across the line, but that isn't allowed. He was credited with second, one lap down, since pushing the car was a one-lap penalty. Petty was a lap ahead of Parsons, making him still able to claim second.

"When I went up on him, he had to turn left. If he didn't, he was going to run head-on into the wall," Petty said years later. "When he did, I think he hit the wall anyway. That got my car sideways and I finally spun. He came down through the grass into the infield. A car came down pit road that he hit that straightened him out. If it hadn't been for that, he would have hit the inside guard rail. Then he wouldn't have won the race because neither one of us could have got going."

The story of that famous race was passed down to Petty's son Kyle, who saw a difference in the way drivers of that era handled themselves.

"Richard Petty thought David Pearson was a great race car driver, and he thought Bobby Allison was a great race car driver, and [Buddy] Baker and those guys, and he had a lot of respect for their ability," Kyle Petty once said. "When they got into each other, they didn't jump out and mouth like we do today. They just didn't think about it because they knew they had to go back and race against each other the next week. They were all pretty decent friends."

RICHARD PETTY vs. DAVID PEARSON

	Petty	Pearson
Races Started	1,184	574
Wins	200	105
Top Fives	555	301
Poles	126	113
Winnings	$8,541,218	$2,836,224

PETTY vs. PEARSON at DAYTONA

1966 Daytona 500: Petty First, Pearson Third
1971 Daytona 500: Petty First, Pearson Fourth
1976 Daytona 500: Pearson First, Petty Second
1969 Firecracker 400: Pearson Fourth, Petty Fifth
1972 Firecracker 400: Pearson First, Petty Second
1973 Firecracker 400: Pearson First, Petty Second
1974 Firecracker 400: Pearson First, Petty Second
1977 Firecracker 400: Petty First, Pearson Fourth
1978 Firecracker 400: Pearson First, Petty Fourth
1980 Firecracker 400: Pearson Second, Petty Fifth

In February 1979, much of America was caught in a blizzard that pressed life into slow motion from the Rocky Mountains to the East Coast. On race weekend, millions were stuck in their homes, hostages of the snow and ice.

But for NASCAR and the ratings people at CBS, the weather was perfect.

That Sunday marked the first live, flag-to-flag televised coverage of the sport of auto racing. It was a weekend that, because viewers were trapped inside with their televisions, would serve as an introduction to the sport for those outside of the Deep South unfamiliar with this activity of fast cars turning left for money.

The event, however, ended up doing more than providing a broadcast that drew national interest. It showed the sport's other side, where tempers flare and fists fly.

The ending was a fight to the finish and a fight after it.

Richard Petty was running 15 seconds behind Cale Yarborough and Donnie Allison, who were battling for the lead and ended up in a wreck, allowing Petty to slip through for the victory ahead of Darrell Waltrip.

Allison, who led most of the day, and Yarborough, the defending Winston Cup champion and 1977 winner of the 500, were the favorites. Allison came from one lap down and Yarborough came from three down following a spin on Lap 32. As the two entered the backstretch on the last lap, Yarborough tried to slide under Allison, but Allison slipped down and blocked his move. Yarborough ran out of room and put all four tires in the dirt, then came back onto the track and collided with Allison.

The cars stuck together, crashed into the Turn 3 wall, and slid down the banking into the infield.

Ken Squier of CBS Sports was telling the nation: "It all comes down to this! Out of Turn 2, Donnie Allison is first! Where will Cale make his move? He comes to the inside! Donnie Allison throws the block! Cale hits him! He slides! Donnie Allison slides! They hit again! They drive into the turn! They're hitting the wall! They're head-on in the wall! They slide to the inside! They're out of it! Who's going to win it?"

Petty was listening to his crew describe it on his radio and led a three-car parade past the wreck site to beat Waltrip by a car length. A. J. Foyt was third. Based on the number of laps completed, Allison was fourth and Yarborough fifth.

Immediately after the checkered flag, Bobby Allison, who finished 11th, went to check on the conditions of Donnie Allison and Yarborough. Yarborough and Bobby Allison argued, and Yarborough took a swing at him. Then Donnie Allison joined in.

The free-for-all was all caught, live across America, by CBS cameras.

Yarborough blamed the Allisons for conspiring against him, even though Bobby's car wasn't near them—it was several hundred yards ahead—on the last lap.

"It's the worst thing I've ever seen in racing," Yarborough said then. "Bobby waited on us to try to block me. I knew how to win the race. Donnie carried me onto the grass. After that, I lost control."

Said Donnie Allison, "I made up my mind that if he was going to pass me, he would have to pass me high.

When he tried to pass me low, he went off the track. He spun and hit me."

Bobby Allison said he stopped on the cool-down lap "to see if they were both OK. I sure didn't block Cale. I was way ahead of him."

The victory was special for Petty in that during the off season, he had 40 percent of his stomach removed in surgery, and he violated doctor's instructions to refrain from racing for three months.

"I told them I was going to race and there wasn't nothin' they could do about that," he said then. "I didn't know what happened on that last lap. I saw the yellow light flash. I radioed my pit crew and asked them where the wreck was. All they said was, 'Go, go, go.' I couldn't believe it when I saw both them cars sittin' in the grass."

The race became known as the day Madison Avenue discovered NASCAR. Apparently, America liked what it saw. The following year, in 1980, the Daytona 500 was seen in 6.1 million homes.

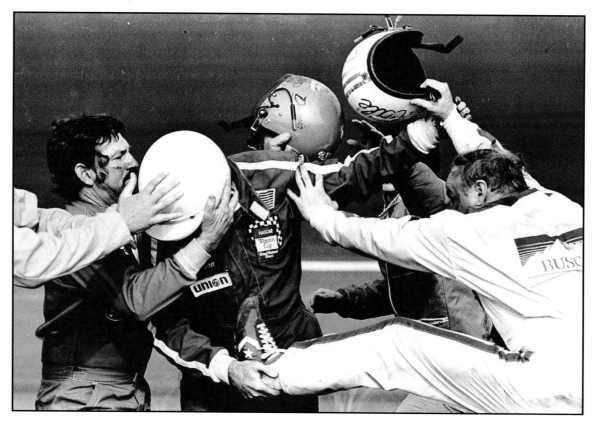

The King and the President Do NASCAR

The other race at Daytona International Speedway, the Pepsi 400, actually was first run in 1959. Richard Petty won three of them, in 1975, 1977 and 1984.

That last one, that's the one Petty calls special.

"Oh, yeah," he said. "I won it on the last lap, in front of the president. That's pretty good."

Ronald Reagan was in the stands that day in Florida—the President watching the King—as Petty won his last race ever, that July 4.

Talk about your midsummer night's dream.

Petty had won his 199th race on May 20, 1984 at Dover. "Normally, a win is just a win," he said then. But this one was special—one away from 200.

Petty's next four races weren't that noteworthy. His best finish was a 13th at Pocono. Maybe he sensed that something special would happen, maybe as a birthday present.

Petty turned 47 on July 2, 1984. He celebrated by qualifying seventh for the Pepsi 400, at 196.692 mph. Cale Yarborough would win the pole. The world was watching. Reagan made the "start your engines" command with a telephone hookup from Air Force One.

Hey, no pressure there.

Yarborough stayed out front until Petty caught him at Lap 14. From then on, it was just the two of them—

they led all but 16 laps the rest of the race. On Lap 128, Petty moved out front, and Yarborough stayed on his rear bumper for the next 30 laps, waiting for a chance to slip around.

With three laps to go, the car of Doug Heveron slid across the track into the grass, went airborne, landed on its roof then flipped back onto its wheels. Heveron was OK, but he had just set up a finishing rush that was one of the best ever.

With a caution about to come out, Petty's and Yarborough's crews were screaming to them on the radio to do something, quick. The two drivers took off like crazy, wanting to set the final running order before the yellow flew.

Side by side they ran, smoke pouring from the backs of their cars, their side panels practically welded together.

Petty zoomed across first, hitting the line about six inches in front of Yarborough.

The yellow flag flew, and the last two laps were driven under caution. Yarborough, obviously unable to win, went to the pits, which enabled Harry Gant to pass him for second.

Petty, for all he did, didn't get to go to Victory Lane. The King was instead taken to the VIP suite to meet the president.

The way the 1987 Winston ended, anything to draw further attention to the way Dale Earnhardt was driving that season was just fine with his fans.

But in reality, what was to become known as the Pass in the Grass really wasn't a pass at all—Earnhardt's No. 3 Chevrolet got tapped into the infield grass, thanks to Bill Elliott, but he never really lost the lead.

Still, it makes for a nice rhyme about a race at Charlotte (now Lowe's) Motor Speedway that was anything but nice.

In the last segment of the three-part race, Earnhardt and Elliott were at each other like crazed alley cats, causing Tim Richmond to say later, "It was worth being in third just to watch the show. It was like bumper cars that last 10 laps … It's not his [Earnhardt's] fault. They're [NASCAR] letting him get away with it."

At one point, Elliott's car hit that of Geoffrey Bodine, spinning him. Elliott claimed Earnhardt hit his rear panel, causing him to tap Bodine. Richmond agreed. Earnhardt said he didn't touch anyone.

On the next lap, Elliott forced Earnhardt off the track, into the grass in the infield, along the front straightaway. Payback? No; two laps later, Elliott got a flat tire, the result—he said—of Earnhardt's hitting his fender in toward the wheel, to where it cut the tire.

Earnhardt won the race, and as he was taking his victory lap, Elliott pulled up behind him and slammed him on the backstretch.

"It was a little bit unsportsmanlike, I thought," Earnhardt said.

Bodine and Richmond, whose cars were the box seats for this show, gave it all a bad review.

"You race hard and you do everything you can, you even rub and bang with people, but you don't try to kill them," Bodine said. "If he [Earnhardt] thinks that's racin' he's sick."

Added Richmond, "I watched that fiasco. I guess no matter how many boos there are, you've gotta keep doing your deal. I think if I got all those boos, I'd have to rethink."

Like him or boo him, the 1987 season belonged to Earnhardt. He won 11 of the 29 races, had 21 top five finishes and 24 top 10s, and won $2,099,243.

He won the Winston Cup title and was the National Motorsports Press Association's driver of the year, a trophy presented to him by Richard Petty.

Someone asked Petty, for whom the NMPA trophy was named, what he would do if he should win his own award someday.

"I'm going to make Dale come back and present it to me," he said.

Allisons Make
Daytona a Family Affair

Davey Allison was in the postrace press conference talking about his hero. "He's always been my hero," he kept saying.

Allison went on and on that day at Daytona International Speedway as if he'd just won the biggest race of his life and his hero had helped him do it.

But he didn't win. Davey Allison was second. Bobby Allison, his father, was first.

It was Valentine's Day 1988, which Davey would call "the happiest

day of my life," and there he was, rambling on, while his father—the race winner—sat calmly nearby and listened to his son chatter.

In the last few laps of the race, it had come down to a father-son duel. What would Bobby do? Would he let his young son, only a few days shy of his 27th birthday, win it? Or would he get himself another victory and teach his son about working hard to earn what you get?

Exiting Turn 4 on the final lap, Bobby Allison floored it and left Davey to finish second.

Lesson learned, again, and for that, Davey would say again, "He's always been my hero."

Growing up in Alabama, the Allisons didn't have a huge savings account to pour into race cars. They mostly pieced parts together with guts, determination and little bit of know-how.

Then they'd take their cars out and whip the guys who had all the money in the world to put into building an engine. They must have done it right: Bobby won 84 Winston Cup races.

Davey Allison, in 1987, was the first rookie to line up out front for Daytona, taking the outside pole. He won Daytona in 1992. But he still counted 1988 as his favorite time ever at the Florida track.

Harry Gant Owns September; Cruel Fate Owns North Wilkesboro

In the high-tech art of building a Winston Cup car, the worst that can happen is for a gadget worth its weight in pocket change to cause the whole ride to go wrong.

It happened to Dale Earnhardt when he hit a piece of scrap metal and cut a tire on the last lap while leading the 1990 Daytona 500.

And it happened to Harry Gant, who was nine laps from making history, in September 1991 at North Wilkesboro.

People had started calling Gant "Mr. September," because he won four consecutive Winston Cup races that month, as well as two Busch Series events, with the Winston Cup streak tying the modern-era record.

Gant won at Darlington, Richmond, Dover and Martinsville.

Then, something unpredictable happened on the way around North Wilkesboro Speedway in the Tyson Holly Farms 400 on the last weekend of the month.

Dale Earnhardt entered the weekend leading the points race, and with only five races to go, he was hop-ing to increase his 59-point lead over Ricky Rudd.

But Earnhardt spent much of the day tagging behind Gant, who led 359 of the 400 laps, and it looked as if Mr. September was about to put another sentence in the record book.

However, with fewer than a dozen laps to go, Gant was victimized by Murphy's Law.

A 10-cent brake part broke on his car. "With 10 laps to go, I had no brakes. Nothing," Gant said later.

"Before long, Dale caught me, and I had to let him go or wreck him. I don't do people like that."

With four and a half miles to go, Earnhardt sped by Gant and won by 1.5 seconds, his fourth win of the season. He'd finish the year with his fifth Winston Cup Championship.

Gant ended 1991 at a career-high fourth in points, with five victories, one pole, 15 top fives and 17 top 10s. He also had the most laps led, with 1,684. His Winston Cup career lasted from 1973 to 1994.

Bruton Smith and H. A. "Humpy" Wheeler are known for their ideas. So when they devised a plan to run NASCAR races at night, people got curious.

The owner and president of Charlotte (now Lowe's) Motor Speedway hired MUSCO Lighting of Oskaloosa, Iowa, to develop a lighting process that uses mirrors to simulate daylight without causing shadows and without the use of view-blocking light poles.

The 1,200-fixture permanent system cost $1.7 million and was installed in 1992.

This bright idea was put to the test in May, 1993, when Charlotte became the first superspeedway to host night racing.

The Coca-Cola 600 lived up to its prerace hype, with Dale Earnhardt being at his intimidating best and a young kid named Jeff Gordon giving a preview of what he would become.

As 162,000 fans watched, Earnhardt drove his No. 3 car like a souped-up dune buggy through a free-for-

all Baja 1000, dodging, nudging, making passing room where none existed.

"Had Houdini been there," one newspaper columnist wrote, "he might have whistled and whooped and stomped his feet for Dale Earnhardt, and then sidled up beside him and said 'How'd you do that?'"

Earnhardt was penalized twice, once for 15 seconds for breaking the rules—"Was I going too fast on pit road?" he slyly asked later—and once for rough driving, when he was given a one-lap slap on the wrist because, somehow, the car of Greg Sacks spun into the wall, across the track and into the grass when Earnhardt may or may not have been near his bumper. "I don't think I nudged him," Earnhardt explained.

At any rate, Earnhardt lost about three miles for doing things his way. When the green flag came out on Lap 335, following the caution caused by the Earnhardt-Sacks case, Earnhardt was about a mile and a half be-

That's when Houdini became his co-pilot, and he began weaving and cutting through and beckoning excuse me, pardon me, to the field until he was in front. He led the final 39 of 400 laps and finished 4.1 seconds ahead of runner-up Jeff Gordon.

"I'm really excited about winning the first 600 to finish under the lights," Earnhardt said. "It's history, and it'll always be special."

What did he think about the late start time? "They can start 'em whenever they like," he said. "I'll finish them."

Dale Jarrett was third, Ken Schrader fourth and Ernie Irvan fifth.

Gordon, a 21-year-old rookie, started 21st and did his own little magic trick after missing a pit and being penalized 15 seconds. He was a lap off the lead and in 15th place on Lap 223 but managed to wrangle through to second place.

Said Gordon's car owner, Rick Hendrick: "He's got a lot of Dale in him."

Indianapolis Motor Speedway had always been a place for open-wheel cars, zipping around the famed 2.5-mile track at unnerving speeds. But on August 24, 1994, the stock cars came to town, and the show brought along a hometown favorite, Jeff Gordon.

Gordon, who spent much of his childhood in nearby Pittsboro, Indiana, had only won one NASCAR race, the Coca-Cola 600 at Charlotte, earlier in the season.

This one in Indianapolis, three days after his 23rd birthday, would prove to be the second.

More than 300,000 fans showed up for the Brickyard 400, the first NASCAR race at the historic track.

Gordon spent much of the final 20 laps battling veteran Ernie Irvan bumper to bumper, but with four laps remaining in the 160-lap race, Irvan stumbled into the pits with a flat tire.

That put Gordon in a race to the finish with Brett Bodine, whom he beat by .53 seconds.

"Me and Ernie were really working on each other," Gordon said. "I drove as hard as I could. If he hadn't had the flat, we probably would have come across the finish line side by side. Our cars were very equal."

Gordon, who started third, averaged 131.931 miles per hour despite several cautions. He earned $613,000.

For the whole season, Gordon won more than any other driver on the circuit—$1,607,010. He ended up with seven top five finishes and 14 top 10s.

Gordon would go on to win the Brickyard two more times—in 1998 and in 2001.

But the first time, in his first try, was the most exciting.

"Oh, my God," Gordon shouted over the radio to his crew, as he crossed the finish line. "I did it! I did it!"

"He's got a knack for winning the big races," one sportswriter wrote. "He's just so talented, probably above everybody else on the circuit."

Ernie Irvan—One More Time Around

On August 20, 1994, Ernie Irvan's race car crashed into the wall at Michigan International Speedway and left him with a 10 percent chance of survival. He was unconscious for two days and suffered severe eye, brain and chest injuries.

But after spending several weeks in the hospital and missing 14 months of being in the driver's seat, Irvan, wearing an eye patch, returned for the last three races of the 1995 season, starting with North Wilkesboro—where he said he could hear the crowd cheering for him above the roar of the engines.

Then, in 1996, he did the impossible. He went to New Hampshire and won the Jiffy Lube 300.

Irvan started sixth and led several times for

brief stretches. His last pit was on Lap 244, when he pulled in for two tires and fuel. Dale Jarrett was second, Ricky Rudd third, Jeff Burton fourth and Robert Pressley fifth—and they were almost glad not to have won.

"I'm not sure I'd have been more happy if I'd have won," Jarrett said.

Said Burton, "It's pretty special to see the 28 car win with all he had to go through."

But Irvan had believed in himself all along. "I never had any doubt in my mind that I could do it again, from the time I started testing," he said after the race. "I had a lot of injuries, but I got hooked up with a lot of good doctors."

On August 20, 1999, exactly five years after his life-threatening crash, Irvan hit the wall at Michigan again. This time, it was

a bruised lung and minor head injury. But it was enough—at age 40, Irvan announced his retirement.

He had broken all the rules by coming back from the first crash and winning again in a race car. It was time to go.

"Everything that I've done and been able to accomplish in the sport has made me decide that the smartest thing I can do is look to the future and retire," he said two weeks later, when he made his announcement at Darlington.

"There's nothing the doctors have actually told me. They did say another accident like the one I had earlier probably would be detrimental to me living a wholesome life. It's something that brings tears to my eyes to know that I'm never going to drive a Winston Cup car again."

The 1996 Jiffy Lube 300
At New Hampshire International Raceway
(Cars finishing on the lead lap)

Position	Car	Driver	Sponsor	Make	Laps	Points	Bonus	Money
1	28	Ernie Irvan	Texaco/Havoline	Ford	300	180	5	$112,625
2	88	Dale Jarrett	Ford Quality Care	Ford	300	175	5	$59,725
3	10	Ricky Rudd	Tide	Ford	300	170	5	$49,825
4	99	Jeff Burton	Exide Batteries	Ford	300	160		$31,600
5	33	Robert Pressley	Skoal Bandit	Chevrolet	300	160	5	$34,825
6	5	Terry Labonte	Kellogg's Corn Flakes	Chevrolet	300	155	5	$42,733
7	2	Rusty Wallace	Miller	Ford	300	146		$30,725
8	25	Ken Schrader	Budweiser	Chevrolet	300	147	5	$27,025
9	30	Johnny Benson	Pennzoil	Pontiac	300	143	5	$27,825
10	21	Michael Waltrip	Citgo	Ford	300	134		$30,025
11	16	Ted Musgrave	The Family Channel	Ford	300	135	5	$26,425
12	3	Dale Earnhardt	GM Goodwrench Service	Chevrolet	300	132	5	$32,225

Dale Wins Daytona—Finally

The greatest finish of the greatest race did not end in a bumper-to-bumper duel, or in a last-second pass, or in any other great, accelerating fashion.

It ended under caution.

Dale Earnhardt won the Daytona 500 on February 15, 1998, in his 20th attempt at the Big One after, in years past, every possible misfortune had landed on his No. 3 Goodwrench Cheverolet.

"I have been passed on the last lap, I have run out of gas and I have cut a tire," Earnhardt said of previous Daytonas.

He also had gone 59 races—nearly two seasons—without a win anywhere.

But on this day, the seven-time NASCAR Winston Cup champion would win. He won after stopping for fuel and right-side tires with 30 laps to go. And he won after the yellow flag came out on Lap 199, following a collision between drivers Jimmy Spencer and John Andretti. He also won in the third fastest time ever, averaging 172.712 miles per hour.

"It was my time," he said later. "I don't care how we won it, but we won it."

For that, he got a standing ovation from 180,000 spectators. As he drove to Victory Lane, his progress was slowed, like a king's chariot in a parade, as more than 100 crew members from other teams jumped the pit wall to congratulate him, to touch the car, to touch the arm of the man at the wheel.

Later, Earnhardt, who led five times for 107 laps, admitted that even The Intimidator could surrender to emotion.

"I cried a little bit in the race car on the way to the checkered flag," he said. "Well, maybe not cried, but at least my eyes watered up."

Following the collision on Lap 199, the yellow and white flags flew simultaneously. Whoever got there first would win. Earnhardt used the lapped Ford of Rick Mast as a pick-me-up and crossed the line as thousands in the grandstand cheered.

His celebration, his reaction to this moment in time, the biggest racing moment of his life, led him to create … doughnuts.

Earnhardt pulled into the infield grass. He spun his car around, gunning the engine and holding the brake, until the skid marks looked as if he had landscaped a "3" in the turf.

Fans rushed from the stands to, literally, get a piece of the action. They brought their coolers for storage, and they snatched up swatches of grass and dirt and history, to stow away for souvenirs.

The victory was worth $1,059,150, the first time in Winston Cup series racing that the winner's share topped $1 million. Bobby Labonte was second, Jeremy Mayfield third, Ken Schrader fourth, Rusty Wallace fifth and Ernie Irvan sixth.

Later, in the press box, Earnhardt pulled a toy monkey out of his shirt. "I'm here!" he shouted. "And I finally got that monkey off my back!"

It was, overall, Earnhardt's 31st win at the Daytona Beach track, taking in all the other contests run there over the years. It was, though, the only one that mattered.

DALE IN DAYTONA

Year	Start	Finish
1979	10	8
1980	32	4
1981	7	5
1982	10	36
1983	3	35
1984	29	2
1985	18	32
1986	4	14
1987	13	5
1988	6	10
1989	8	3
1990	2	5
1991	4	5
1992	3	9
1993	4	2
1994	2	7
1995	2	2
1996	1	2
1997	4	31
1998	2	1

Earnhardt Takes Critics for a Ride

On November 12, 1995, Dale Earnhardt set the Winston Cup race record at Atlanta Motor Speedway at 163.633 miles per hour.

On March 12, 2000, he demonstrated his ability to master the 1.54-mile oval with a thrilling performance in the Cracker Barrel 500.

Fans had been complaining that races were getting boring, that it was more follow-the-leader than gas-and-pass. And Chevrolet had been complaining that its 2000 Monte Carlos had unfair restrictions placed on them, making them aerodynamically inferior.

But on this Sunday, at least for a day, that changed.

Chevrolet drivers were allowed to extend their air dams by two inches, and five of the top 10 spots ended up being Chevrolets.

It was a driver in a Pontiac, however, that gave Earnhardt his co star for the afternoon's performance.

The race had 30 lead changes among 17 drivers, with Earnhardt taking the lead for good on Lap 306 of the 325-lap event. Bobby Labonte, in a Pontiac, repeatedly challenged him and twice in the final 10 laps tried to pass.

On the last lap, Labonte came off Turn 4 and pulled even with Earnhardt's Chevrolet, and they raced side by side to the finish.

In one of the closest finishes in NASCAR history, Earnhardt was declared the winner by 0.010 seconds.

"It definitely wasn't a boring race," he said afterward. It was Earnhardt's ninth win at Atlanta. Labonte had won four of the past seven races at the track prior to the Cracker Barrel.

"I was racing for all I could get and for all it would do," Earnhardt said. "I was just driving the car as hard as I could go and giving it everything I had … It wasn't time to take it easy."

Mark Martin (Ford) was third, Steve Park (Chevrolet) fourth and Joe Nemechek (Chevrolet) fifth. The second five were Chad Little (Ford), Todd Bodine (Chevrolet), Ward Burton (Pontiac), Jeff Gordon (Chevrolet) and Bill Elliott (Ford).

"NASCAR is doing a better job each week to make the cars competitive," Earnhardt said. "And I think it showed this week with all three makes being competitive and racing well.

"It was pretty competitive, I thought."

Harold Brasington's Egg-Shaped Field of Dreams

In the fall of 1949, local businessman Harold Brasington looked out across a cotton field on the west side of Darlington, South Carolina, and where most people would have seen dirt, cattle and a minnow-filled watering hole, Brasington saw speed.

He envisioned stock cars racing around a paved superspeedway. He saw grandstands filled with adoring fans, watching stars in cars.

His friends thought he was nuts, had thought it since 1933 when Brasington came home from Indianapolis and mentioned it would be nice if tiny Darlington could have a racetrack, too.

Brasington took to the seat of bulldozers and grading equipment and did some of the work himself. Bucket by bucket, dirt was pushed around to shape a one-and-a-fourth-mile superspeedway right there in the Pee Dee River Valley. Brasington wanted a perfect oval, but the farmer who owned the pond refused to give it up, so the pavement in what is Turns 3 and 4 was rerouted around it and Ramsey's Pond was safe.

Thus, Darlington became a track of skill. Others, later, would be bigger, have more grandstands, be more modernized. But Darlington, plain and simple, is built to test drivers, as its nickname implies:"The track too tough to tame."

The 1.366-mile oval has equal 1,229-foot front and back straightaways, with 25-degree bankings in Turns 1 and 2 and 23-degree bankings in Turns 3 and 4. The width of Turns 1 and 2 is 79 feet, but the width in Turns 3 and 4 is only 62 feet.

Because of the layout, expansion is difficult. In 1997, the configuration was changed so that the southern straightaway became the frontstretch, to accommodate a new high-rise grandstand. But other than that, it's pretty much stuck as is.

Which, some say, could put Darlington in a dilemma, with NASCAR rapidly expanding its marketability.

"Personally speaking, I think Darlington has such tradition that it would be a shame to pull a race away from there and take it to some other area," car owner Larry McClure said once."Darlington is such a good racetrack and a good race for the fans."

Darlington has two dates on the Winston Cup schedule, one in March and the Southern 500 the first weekend of September.

As the sport gravitates more toward high-tech and high commercial appeal, Darlington remains, for now, a piece of what it was like back when a man could stand in a rural field, see speed, and have people think the whole thing was a crazy dream.

The Houses That Big Bill Built

In 1934, William France set out to move his family from Washington to Miami, Florida. But along the way, the family car broke down in Daytona Beach.

France, a mechanic, could have fixed the car and gone on, but he liked what he saw and stayed where he was.

And where he was became the birthplace of NASCAR.

William Henry Getty France, known as "Big Bill," was born in Washington, D.C., on September 26, 1909. At age 17, he built a race car with a wooden body covered with canvas. He worked at gas stations and automotive repair shops, and raced his car on little, neighboring dirt tracks. The established racers of the time were racing at the Baltimore-Washington Speedway in nearby Laurel, Maryland, and he hoped to some day be able to afford to join them.

He married Anne Bledsoe, a nurse, and they had a son, William Clifton. A few years later, with $25 in his pocket, $75 in the bank and a tool box in the trailer, Bill France and his family headed south. At Ormond Beach just north of Daytona, France drove down to the beach and on along the water's edge to the main pier at Daytona. But going back across the bridge to the mainland, the car broke down.

France already had made up his mind to stay, anyway. He rented a three-bedroom bungalow for $13.50 a month and got a job at a car dealership.

In 1937, he announced he would put on a beach race. The course went one and a half miles down the sand, then turned and went back up the beach and turned again at the north end, a distance of 3.2 miles.

France won the 1938 event and took home $100. In 1947, he organized about 10 races throughout the South in what he called the National Championship Stock Car Circuit—which used mostly family sedans.

Anne France handled the points fund, and when the first season ended, they had $3,000 in payoffs to divide among drivers. Racing was becoming popular, so France called some of his car buddies for a meeting.

And on December 14, 1947, in the roof garden of the Streamline Hotel in Daytona Beach, the National Association of Stock Car Auto Racing was born.

Tracks and drivers were eager to join. In 1949, France organized a late-model, strictly stock race at the old Charlotte Speedway, near what is now Pineville. The purse was huge: about $6,000.

In 1959, France opened a 2.5-mile tri-oval called Daytona International Speedway.

France was known as a tough ruler in NASCAR until in 1972 he turned the operation over to his son, Bill.

"He ran NASCAR with an iron fist," Bobby Allison once said. "There were no arguments, no back talk, nothing. If you were going to race NASCAR, you were going to do it his way and you weren't going to say anything unless you were asked. But I felt like he was fair. Big Bill told me a benevolent dictatorship was needed because a democratic deal wouldn't allow things to go ahead and progress."

France also built the track at Talladega, Alabama, and had controlling interests in Darlington (S.C.) Raceway, Watkins Glen in New York and Tucson Raceway Park in Arizona.

Bill France, Sr. died June 6, 1992, at age 82 at his home in Ormond Beach, after a long battle with Alzheimer's. He was buried at the First Baptist Church in Daytona Beach.

Said Junior Johnson, "They say Richard Petty's the King, Dale Earnhardt's the Iron Man, Cale Yarborough's the Wild Man and Darrell's [Waltrip] one thing or another, but Bill France, Sr. is the hero of this sport. He's what got us here."

The First Daytona:
500 Miles, Four Days

The inaugural Daytona 500 was held on February 22, 1959. The finish of the race was three days later.

Lee Petty, driving a 1959 Oldsmobile '88 (he switched between Oldsmobiles and Chryslers, depending on what he though would work best at a particular track), crossed the finish line in a dead heat with Johnny Beauchamp.

As 41,000 fans watched from the stands of the new superspeedway, two miles inland from the packed beach sands where the early Daytona races had been run, NASCAR declared Beauchamp the winner.

Petty protested.

Since this was long before videotaping and instant replay, organizers had to rely on individual snapshots and news stations' accounts to figure this one out and double-check the results.

Three days later—actually, 61 hours after the checkered flag—NASCAR based its decision on newsreel footage and declared Petty the winner ... by two feet.

"There wasn't any driver better than Lee Petty in his day," Junior Johnson said in 2000 after Petty died at age 86 of complications from surgery.

"There might have been more colorful drivers, but when it came down to winning a race, he had as much as anyone I've ever seen."

At the time of his Daytona victory, Petty was the defending Grand National (now Winston Cup) champion. He would win his second of three consecutive titles in 1959 by a 1,830-point margin over second-place finisher Cotton Owens.

Petty would win 55 times in his career, and in 1949 he founded what would become Petty Enterprises with his sons, Richard and Maurice.

"We never had anything vicious on the track," Johnson said.

"If he could get in a hole, he got in it ... When the race was over, he hooked up and went home."

Buddy Baker Learns to Fly

Buddy Baker once said, "It killed my pride if I didn't run up front. And if you didn't win, it was like being the second man to discover America."

Baker had his moment to run up front where others had yet to travel, on March 24, 1970, when he was the first driver to exceed 200 miles per hour on a closed course. Baker, born Wylie Baker Jr. on January 25, 1941 in Florence, South Carolina, had raced since age 17, first in the long-gone convertible division on tracks in Columbia, S.C. His first big win was the National 500 in 1967 at Charlotte Motor Speedway.

But on his history-making day, Baker was in Talladega, testing his Dodge Daytona for the Alabama 500.

He circled the track at 200.447 miles per hour. No wonder the son of famous driver Buck Baker was nicknamed "Leadfoot."

Baker was known for going fast on the fastest tracks. He won the Winston 500 in 1975, 1976 and 1980 and the Talladega 500 in 1975. He won the Daytona 500 in 1980 and the Firecracker 400 in 1983.

In all, he ran 688 NASCAR Winston Cup races, winning 19 of them. He finished 202 races in the top five and 299 races in the top 10. He took 40 poles, and he took home $3.6 million.

But for all that, he can say he was known for speed. When he won the Daytona 500 from the pole in 1980, he set a race record of 177.602 miles per hour, making it the first Daytona run in less than three hours.

And one day in March 1970, in Talladega, Alabama, he set the standard for the future when he clocked the first 200.

In the early 1970s, Junior Johnson had an idea, one of his more innovative ones.

NASCAR's Grand National series was having money problems, and president Bill France Sr. mentioned to Johnson that the sport might need a little help in the bankroll department.

Johnson had lost his sponsorship from the R.J. Reynolds Tobacco Company in 1969 and already was on his way from his home in the North Carolina hills to nearby Winston-Salem to ask for a check from Winston to please sponsor his car.

A 1972 ruling by Congress said cigarette companies could not advertise their products on television, so it coincidentally happened that R. J. Reynolds was on the lookout for another venue.

France smelled jackpot.

Johnson smelled free ride.

"Junior's scheme was to get money from them to sponsor his car," said a long-time NASCAR writer, "so he goes in there asking for about $500,000. They said, 'We have $50 million. Let's go see Bill France about this.' And that's how R. J. Reynolds got involved."

The two companies worked a deal, and from 1972 on, the Grand National Series became known as Winston Cup. During its first year, Winston established a points fund for drivers worth $100,000. At the end of that year, Richard Petty claimed the champion's $40,000 slice at the Plaza Hotel in Daytona Beach. In 2001, the winner's portion was $3.4 million out of a $13 million prize fund.

"Prior to Winston coming on board, we really had no title sponsor, and it was just called Grand National racing," said Eddie Wood, owner of Wood Brothers Racing. "After they came on board, and even now, they brought the purses. That created a lot of stability."

Since that day Junior Johnson walked in asking for a sponsor, Winston has given more than $70 million to points funds.

Winston and R. J. Reynolds dipped into other sports on wheels, too, supporting the National Hot Rod Association's drag racing series, top fuel dragsters and Pro Stock Motorcycle events.

"You race every week because of that point fund," Wood once said. "Some races seem bigger than others, and I guess they are as far as purse money and exposure go, but each race pays the same amount of points. That's what it's all about. Every week after the race ends you're looking at that rundown to see where you are in points because at the end of the year you want to be in that top 25."

Since 1985, Winston also has had its signature race: The Winston has been run each year since then at Lowe's Motor Speedway.

Cale Yarborough hits a triple

Cale Yarborough's Winston Cup career spanned four decades, from 1957 to 1988. During that time, he won 83 races and had 70 pole positions.

He also became the only driver in history to win three championships in a row.

Yarborough was Winston Cup champion in 1976, 1977 and 1978 while driving for NASCAR legend Junior Johnson, who became a car owner when his own driving career ended.

Yarborough won nine races in 1976 and nine in 1977, steering a Chevrolet, and won $387,173 in each of those years. In 1978, the team switched to Oldsmobiles, and Yarborough won 10 races and brought in $530,751. That's 28 out of a possible 90 races—and he finished second 18 times.

Many drivers have managed to win back-to-back titles in the modern era, including Jeff Gordon (1997, 1998), Dale Earnhardt (1986, 1987; 1990, 1991; 1993, 1994), Darrell Waltrip (1981, 1982) and Richard Petty (1974, 1975).

But for those three years, Yarborough was untouchable. In 1976, he raked in 4,644 points, 195 ahead of second-place finisher Richard Petty. In 1977, he reached 5,000 points, the first driver to do so, and beat Petty by 386. In 1978, he was 474 points ahead of Bobby Allison, with a total of 4,841.

In '77 and '78, his points totals were high enough for him to clinch the Winston Cup title with two races remaining in the season.

Yarborough also knew what it was like to finish second in the title chase. He did that in 1973, behind Benny Parsons; in 1974 behind Petty; and in 1980, behind Dale Earnhardt.

But that was the end of the storybook, as Yarborough did not finish in the top 10 again after 1980 through his career-ending season in 1988.

Year to Winston Cup Champ

There were 31 Winston Cup races run in 1980. Dale Earnhardt wasn't on the pole for any of them.

In 1979, the upstart from Kannapolis, North Carolina, had been Rookie of the Year, with one win, 11 top five finishes, 17 top 10s and four poles. But 1980 was a whole new deal, literally. In January, Earnhardt announced he had signed a five-year agreement with Osterlund Racing, whose cars had taken him to his rookie milestone. "Talk about job security," the 28-year-old said. "I've got it."

He proved his worth immediately, winning the Busch Clash in Daytona in February on national television.

He would go on to win five races, have 19 top five finishes, 23 top 10s and increase his bank account by $588,926. Dale Earnhardt would advance from Rookie of the Year to Winston Cup champion—the only second-year driver in the 31-year history of Grand National racing to take that title.

And, as he would do so often in his career, Earnhardt gave credit to his father, Ralph, who had died in 1973 but taught him the rules of the game.

"We were lucky, and I really believe we had some help from a pretty high source," Earnhardt said.

Earnhardt began his championship season by winning the Atlanta 500 in March over a young Rusty Wallace. He then won the Valleydale Southeastern 500 at Bristol a few weeks later, 8.7 seconds ahead of Darrell Waltrip.

He took his third victory in July at Nashville—where he set a race record of 93.811 miles per hour on the .596-mile oval, two months after his crew chief, Jake Elder, had quit the team.

Win number four came at Martinsville in September with a new crew chief, Doug Richert, giving him a 105-point lead over Cale Yarborough in the title chase.

The fifth win came just 12 miles from home, at Charlotte Motor Speedway (now Lowe's), when he won the

National 500 in front of 75,000 fans. "This is the best win, winning here before so many hometown friends and fans," he said.

The victory put him 115 points ahead of Yarborough and paid him $49,050, the most ever for a Winston Cup race.

When it was over, when the title was his, Earnhardt took two of his brothers on a party trip to Las Vegas. One cross-county trip; one big celebration before getting back to work.

Said Earnhardt, "The two years I've been on the Winston Cup circuit, many of the veterans have good-naturedly called me 'Boy.' Now, several of 'em, including Junior Johnson, have offered congratulations and called me 'Champ.'"

Bill Elliott's Million Dollar Paycheck

They started calling him "Million Dollar Bill," and his likeness was placed on fake money.

By winning the Southern 500 at Darlington International Raceway in South Carolina on September 1, 1985, Bill Elliott became the first winner of the Winston Million, a $1 million bonus offered by R.J. Reynolds Tobacco Co. to any driver who won three of the "Big Four" races in one year.

Elliott also won the Daytona 500 and Winston 500. He came up short in the World 600 that May, when his Ford Thunderbird developed brake problems.

The victory at Darlington's 1.366-mile oval gave Elliott the sport's largest single-day payoff—$1,053,725, with $53,725 coming from the race purse of $410,000.

Of course, it was a money-making year already for the 29-year-old from Dawsonville, Georgia. The South-

ern 500 was his 10th victory in 20 starts that year and gave him a single-season earnings total of $1,857,243.

But the finish was a little tight.

Elliott, who started from the pole, won the 367-lap race by six one-hundredths of a second over Cale Yarborough's Thunderbird. He barely got past a spinning Dale Earnhardt on Lap 318 ("I don't know how close I was because I had my eyes closed when I went by," he said), then slipped by Yarborough on Lap 324 when Yarborough's power steering hose broke, releasing a fountain of liquid and steam ("I closed my eyes on that one, too").

"It was like driving a freight train the rest of the race," Yarborough said. "All I could do was steer it and guide it."

The victory was Elliott's 14th of his career, all of which came on superspeedways of a mile or longer. The

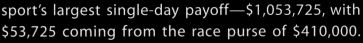

Southern 500 win, being his 10th superspeedway title of the season, tied him with the record set by David Pearson in 1973.

There were 14 caution flags during the race, which ran in front of a crowd estimated at 68,000. Geoffrey Bodine was third, followed a lap down by Neil Bonnett and Ron Bouchard.

Money-wise, Elliott got another footnote in the record books: His one-day earnings surpassed the previous mark of $500,000, which was Danny Sullivan's take from the $3 million purse at the 1985 Indianapolis 500.

Bill Elliott Shows How Fast Talladega Can Go

The track in Alabama is all about speed. The 2.66-mile tri-oval just down the road from Birmingham has seen some fast cars. In March of 1974, Buddy Baker circled the loop at more than 200 miles per hour, the first to break that barrier.

Then, on April 20, 1987, Bill Elliott set the land speed record for qualifying that still stands there—212.809 miles per hour. Of course, that was before NASCAR decided to mandate restrictor plate usage at superspeedways.

But in May 1990, Elliott set the post-restrictor plate qualifying record, too, at 199.388 miles per hour.

"I was hoping we'd run faster," Elliott said, a few years later, of the 212 record. "I thought we had a car capable of running faster than that. Talladega had the capability of running a lot faster. I went over there in a car that we did for Ford for Lynn St. James at that time, and I think I ran 218, and it had the potential to run even faster, and the track had potential for more.

"Unrestricted, these cars today, with the technology they've got today, they'd be running in the 220s relatively easy."

In May 1987, NASCAR decided Talladega's speeds needed to be regulated after Bobby Allison's incredible crash sent him airborne and ripped out 150 feet of a 15-foot-high fence.

"The problem is that Talladega is a place where the restrictor plate forces you into doing things you shouldn't be doing," Elliott said after Allison's wreck led to a mandatory slow-down. "You start cutting people off. People take it for a while, the guy gets mad, and he ain't going to take it anymore. It puts you in a bad situation.

"That's the one thing that's always tough about going to Talladega, especially in today's scenario."

Whatever the opinion is of restrictor plates, their use means Elliott's qualifying record could stand for a long, long time.

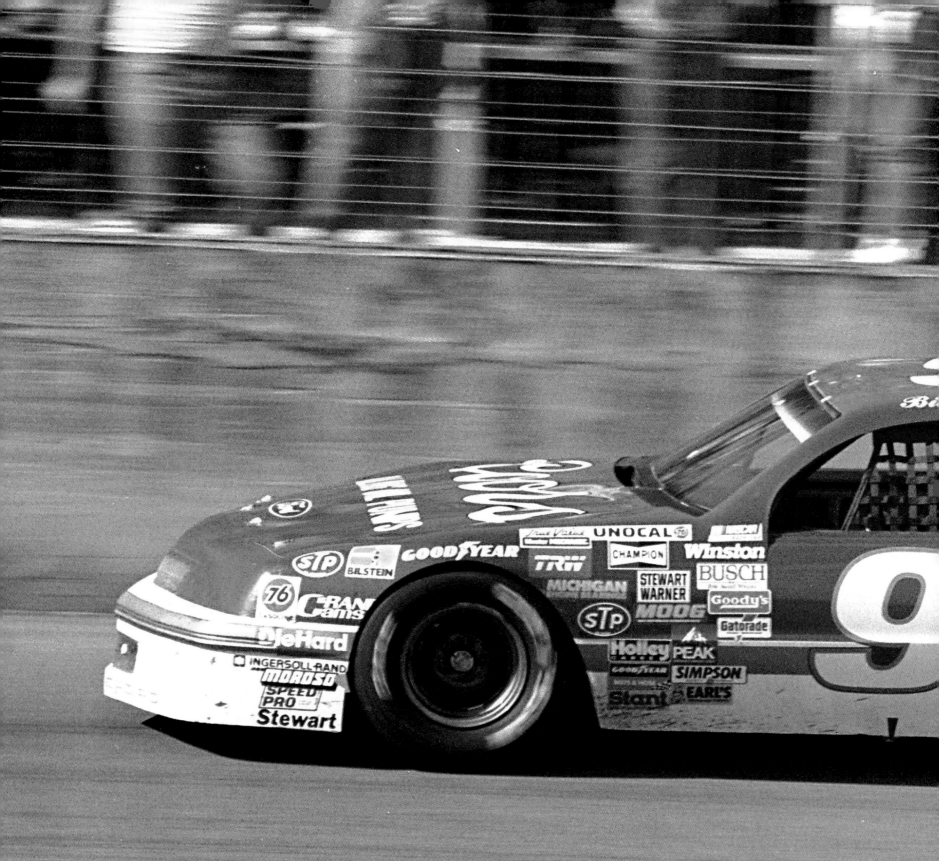

Bobby Allison's Terror Brings On Restrictor Plates

In the complex setup of a 3,000-pound race car, one little device has caused the largest uproar.

Restrictor plates. Drivers either hate them, or just don't like them.

"It's not racin'," Dale Earnhardt once said. "It's the wrong thing to do."

A restrictor plate is a square piece of metal about the size of an adult's hand. Its purpose is simple: Placed between a car's intake manifold and carburetor, it limits the amount of air that is able to reach the carburetor. The less air that gets in, the lower the temperature of the burning fuel and the lower the horsepower. Thus, cars with restrictor plates go slower.

Whatever their opinion, drivers can look to Bobby Allison's horrific crash at Talladega, Alabama, in 1987 as the moment NASCAR finally conceded that speeds had edged beyond safe.

On May 3, 1987, on Lap 21 of the Winston 500 at Alabama International Motor Speedway (now Talladega Super-speedway), Allison was running fifth on the course known as the world's fastest track. He was doing an estimated 205 miles per hour when the right rear tire blew.

The car lifted, and the change in aerodynamics picked up the 3,500-pound Buick and sent it skyward, rear end first, high into the chain-link fence in front of the crowd. Parts of his car sprayed into the stands as the vehicle tore out nine steel uprights and 150 feet of a 15-foot-high fence.

After ripping the fence, the car bounced back into the center of the track, where it narrowly missed the rest of the following stream of cars. When the Buick had ricocheted off the screen, its underside was caught in the fencing, causing the car to peel the fence off like the top of a potato chip can.

Amazingly, no one was seriously injured. Four spectators were hurt, one with possible eye damage who was taken to a hospital in nearby Birmingham. The other three were treated and released.

Seven other cars were damaged, but only two—the cars of Cale Yarborough and Ron Bouchard—couldn't finish the race. Bouchard's car cut a tire, then hit Yarborough's. When another car cut off Yarborough and he braked, Bouchard hit him again, sending both back to the garage.

The race was stopped for two hours, 38 minutes while new fencing was delivered by police escort and installed as the race cars sat single-file along the front straightaway.

When racing resumed, drivers were uninhibited by what happened. No one was hurt, and in drivers' minds, that means everything is OK. Bobby Labonte was clocked later in the race at 207.7 miles per hour.

The Winston 500 was won by Davey Allison, a 26-year-old rookie, who led 101 of the 178 laps. He was just ahead of his 49-year-old father when the wreck happened.

"My heart fainted when I saw Dad in my mirrors," Davey Allison said. "When I saw him, he was already up in the air, sideways, headed for the grandstand. I was afraid he might go into it … When I got back around and saw him crawling out of the car, it lifted my heart back to where it belonged."

Bobby Allison later said he may have run over something, that he felt something bouncing around under the car.

The race had nine caution flags for 39 laps, slowing the average speed to 154.214 miles per hour. But under green, no lap was clocked slower than 200.

NASCAR had to do something. It made restrictor plates mandatory at Talladega and Daytona International Speedway, and for the September 2000 race following the deaths at New Hampshire International Speedway of Kenny Irwin and Adam Petty, it made their use mandatory there, also.

Driver Sterling Marlin said he saw the plates as an advantage for fans. "You didn't see much passing back then. Back when they were going 211 or 212, you just aimed the car and hoped it went where you aimed it," he said.

Following second-round qualifying for the Winston 500 in October 2000 at Talladega, all 43 drivers were summoned to a mandatory meeting at the NASCAR inspection bay.

Thirty-five minutes later, each left holding a new restrictor plate with a 15/16-inch opening, replacing the ones with the one-inch opening they had been using. They had run too fast in qualifying. NASCAR didn't like it.

The wreck that day in May 1987, as chilling and frightening as it was, did not scare Bobby Allison off the track. On July 4 that year, he won the Firecracker 400 at Daytona, breaking a 34-race winless streak.

That victory made him the oldest driver at the time to win a NASCAR race, at 49 years, 7 months, 1 day.

Alan Kulwicki—
Who Would Have Thought?

The 1992 Hooters 500 at Atlanta Motor Speedway could have been the draft for a television miniseries the way it played out, with all its subplots and cast of characters working toward an unlikely season-ending moment.

Alan Kulwicki was the underdog, the one hoping to win the Winston Cup title, but that was against the odds. Kulwicki, from Wisconsin of all places, had shunned big-money offers for his team, instead choosing to do things by himself, as he pleased.

Bill Elliott was the likely hero, driving for the rich and famous Junior Johnson—definitely a title contender.

Davey Allison, the points leader coming in, only needed to finish sixth or higher to win the championship. How hard could that be?

Meanwhile, away from the title chase, Richard Petty was entered for his final Winston Cup race ever. The King was ready to take his crown and go home to the farm in North Carolina.

Also that day, some new kid from Indiana named Jeff Gordon, who, unlike Petty, would never be seen in a cowboy hat, was making his Winston Cup debut.

Episode by episode, the plot evolved toward the surprise ending.

On Lap 253, Ernie Irvan eliminated one subplot when he had a tire go out, and he lost control in front of Rusty Wallace and Allison, who was running sixth. Wallace avoided the mishap, but Irvan got T-boned by Allison and Allison's car was put out of contention.

Elliott and Kulwicki ran 1-2 the rest of the way, the lead changing several times.

Whichever driver led the most laps would be champion—and get a $1 million bonus from Winston.

The whole season—the championship, the bonus, the guy from Wisconsin vs. the guy who drove for Junior Johnson—came down to one lap.

On Lap 310, Kulwicki pitted while he was leading, knowing he had clinched the bonus by leading 103 of the 328 laps. Elliott then gained the lead and drove on to his fifth victory of the season.

But Elliott had only led 102 laps of the race. If he had led one lap that Kulwicki did not, making it 103-102 the other way, Elliott would have gotten the bonus points and they would have tied for season total. If that had happened, Elliott would have won the championship because he had more race victories.

So Elliott won the race but lost the battle, as Kulwicki won the 1992 Winston Cup Championship. By 10 points.

John Andretti Tries for 1,100-mile Day; Tony Stewart Does It

The night before it happened, John Andretti remembers, he didn't worry about his race cars. Instead, he worried about the weather.

Rain in Indianapolis would make his Sunday impossible. Rain in Charlotte, however, would be OK, as long as it was just a little sprinkler.

In May 1994, Andretti was attempting to become the first person to drive in the Indianapolis 500 and Coca-Cola 600 in the same day.

The weather cooperated. When he awoke, it was sunny in Indiana.

"A rain delay in Indianapolis was going to make it really tough to make the start of the race in Charlottte. A rain delay in Charlotte, at least at the start, was going to make it a little easier," he recalled years later.

He started 10th in Indianapolis, and he finished 10th. Then, he ran to a helicopter pad, zoomed to the airport and boarded a plane to Charlotte.

Even the time on the plane was factored into the plans. He had fruit and light food ready for him, as well as two IV bags of saline solution. When he got to North Carolina, he said he "felt pretty good."

He was a few minutes late and had to miss the driver's meeting, which put him at the back of the field.

"It's funny in that not a lot of people took it very seriously when we first talked about doing it," Andretti said. "I guess nobody thought it could be done. I was doing just the one Indy race, the Indianapolis 500, and was with an unsponsored Winston Cup team at the time, too."

When he qualified in Charlotte, the media began to pay attention.

"I was running both because I really wanted to run both," he said. "I don't like them running races without me in them."

Turns out, Andretti wrecked in the 600 and didn't finish the race.

But in May 1999, Tony Stewart did. (Robby Gordon tried a double in 1997 but was rained out in Indianapolis.)

Stewart, who switched to Winston Cup after three years in the Indy Racing League, finished ninth in Indy, then jetted to Charlotte to do it again.

It was a three minute ride to the Indianapolis airport, where Home Depot had a jet waiting for the 65-minute flight to Charlotte. Stewart, who had put on blue jeans, switched to his NASCAR suit, ate a nutrition bar and drank a sports drink on the plane.

But during the last hour of the 600, he felt sick, exhausted. Still, he finished fourth.

When he climbed from his car, his legs collapsed and he leaned on his ride for several minutes, taking fluids.

Finally, he said,

"I'm ready for a nap."

Stewart had done 1,100 miles in 10 hours—the distance of driving from Los Angeles to Denver, with 2,384 left turns.

"We fought hard all day," he said.

John Andretti thought about it again in 2002, but Kyle Petty, CEO of Petty Enterprises and owner of Andretti's cars, decided maybe some other time.

"Kyle and I sat down and talked and decided we'd wait and talk about it in the future," Andretti said. "It's disappointing … It would be an unbelievable year to go back."

However in 2002 Robbie Gordon did complete the 1,100 mile journey. He finished eighth in the Indianapolis 500 and 16th in the Coca Cola 600.

Junior Johnson's Exit Ramp

Junior Johnson, the practically legendary Wilkes County, North Carolina, native personified everything NASCAR was in its infancy but slipped back home to the farm when faced with the escalation of what the sport has become.

In 1965, writer Thomas Wolfe called him "The Last American Hero" for his pure country attitude and lifestyle. Johnson grew up in the Carolina hills and learned to drive by running moonshine. In the late 1940s, he took up racing on little dirt tracks, and he made his Grand National (now Winston Cup) debut in 1953.

Johnson parked his car as a driver in 1966 at age 34, with 50 victories in the bank. But he stayed in the sport to utilize his skills as a mechanic and a businessman. He also was sly enough, according to one longtime racing writer, to rig a race car just short of being caught by NASCAR inspection crews.

Johnson was quite good, the writer insists, at cheating without getting caught.

As a car owner, Junior Johnson watched his race teams rack up more than 100 victories.

Johnson's final race as an owner was at Atlanta in 1995, with Brett Bodine behind the wheel. Seeing how the sport was being towed along by big money and sponsorship, and crew members making demands for their career paths, Johnson stepped back and let it go on without him.

He was content to return to his spacious home and farm back in Wilkes County.

That decision left Bodine in charge of the team, after Bodine did some financial juggling to keep his ride rolling through the 1996 season. Where Johnson was the last of a breed—that of the whiskey hauling, backwoods dirt track drivers of the sport's beginning— Bodine became one of the last of a modern-era breed with Johnson's departure—that of owner-driver.

Earnhardt Survives the Unthinkable Crash

The theory is that if Dale Earnhardt had obeyed the rules, he could have been in much worse shape than he was.

It was July 28, 1997 at Talladega, and Earnhardt was battling Sterling Marlin for the lead when Marlin's car and Ernie Irvan's touched, and Marlin's bumped Earnhardt's and sent the No. 3 Chevrolet into the air on a 200-mile-an-hour flight.

When the car landed, it was on its side—the worst place to be, because if it were to be hit, it wouldn't roll.

"You could look down pit road and have a sense that something had happened and maybe he was dead," said Lowe's Motor Speedway president H. A. "Humpy" Wheeler when asked about the incident later. "The thing we always fear is, 'What if a driver gets hit with his car upside down?' And this one ended up on its side, and no one could survive the kind of wreck he had."

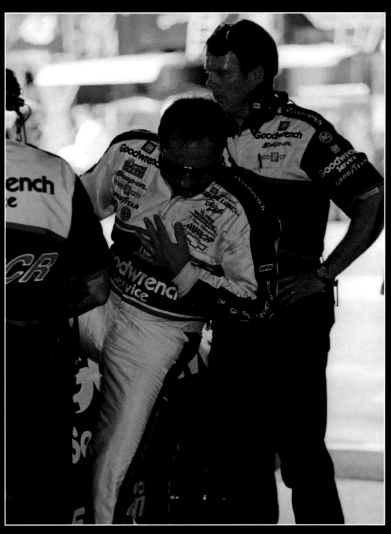

Earnhardt's car was hit, in the roof, by the car of Derrick Cope.

As a hushed crowd watched, safety crews took several long minutes to get Earnhardt out of his car. Incredibly, he walked to the ambulance by himself.

"The reason he survived, and the only reason he survived, is that he did what everyone told him not to do," Wheeler said.

"It's the slouching way he sits in a race car. Also, his seat is rigged up so his head leans toward the outside of the car. The fact that he walked out of that car is phenomenal."

Earnhardt had a broken sternum and collarbone. Three days later, he qualified 12th at Indianapolis for the Brickyard 400. On race day, he hurt too much to drive, but he went six laps anyway.

During a caution period, he pulled in and climbed out. He had proven he could come back but was disappointed he couldn't finish.

Dodge Returns with Hopes of More Glory Days

On May 5, 2000, with cameras clicking and news stations focused on the garage, a new model came out from its proverbial backstage waiting area to make its runway debut.

When the gray Dodge Intrepid R/T race car rolled out at Homestead-Miami Speedway, it marked the first time in more than two decades that Dodge would be a part of Winston Cup racing. The announcement had been made the previous October that Dodge would be back—in time for the 2001 Daytona 500.

On this date in Miami, the gray car had its first rehearsal in front of more than a dozen Dodge dealers and officials from the United Auto Workers union.

"When you start a program and grow it from its infancy to a point where it becomes a reality, it does touch you emotionally," said Lou Patane, vice president of Dodge Motorsports Operations. "And when I see the effort all the people put in from the team side and from the company side to get us to this milestone—and this is only one of many milestones we will accomplish—it does give you a special feeling."

The day also was special for test driver Kyle Petty, whose father, Richard, and grandfather, Lee, were behind

the wheels for many of Dodge's 160 victories decades earlier.

Richard Petty won 27 of his 48 starts in a Dodge in 1967, including 10 in a row. Lee Petty won his 1954 and 1959 titles in a Chrysler. Tim Flock (1955 champion) and Buck Baker (1956) also drove Chryslers.

But no Dodge/Chrysler product had been on top since Richard Petty's title in 1975.

"I wouldn't miss this for the world," Kyle Petty said. "This is a big day for Kyle Petty personally."

Petty Enterprises, Bill Davis Racing and Evernham Motorsports all had announced plans to switch to Dodge cars.

Team owner Ray Evernham, one of the major backers of Dodge's return, liked what he saw the first day. "The fact that we unloaded the car and put it on the track with no problems, and with all the engineering and test systems working as they should, it really is a big accomplishment," he said.

When the car was put back on the hauler, its backers had one thought.

Daytona 2001 was 291 days away.

When that day came, Dodge not only showed up, but Bill Elliott drove his to the pole position.

In all, drivers in Dodges included: Elliott, his teammate Casey Atwood; Kyle Petty, John Andretti and "Buckshot" Jones of Petty Enterprises; Ward Burton and Dave Blaney of Bill Davis Racing; and Sterling Marlin and Jason Leffler of Chip Ganassi Racing.

"All of the hard work and preparation materialized in front of our eyes," said Dodge executive Bob Wildberger, "and the vision of making it to the 2001 Daytona 500 became that much closer."

Earnhardt, Earnhardt and Earnhardt

Dale and Dale Jr. aren't the only Earnhardts to have guided a race car. Kerry, Dale's oldest son, and Kelly, his oldest daughter, also have strapped in.

"I think it was at Nashville Motor Speedway when Dale Jr. and I last ran together in late models," Kerry said in the summer of 2000. "It was exciting. Me and Dale Jr. and Kelly all ended up rac-

ing in that race. We all ended up getting in the same wreck on Lap 2. We were all able to come in and fix our cars and get back out there and race a little bit."

At Michigan that year, on August 20, there would be three Earnhardts: Dad, Dale Jr. and Kerry on the track at the same time.

"My lifelong dream was Winston Cup racing, and it's like an added bonus to have Dad and Dale Jr. in the same race that I'll be racing in," he said prior to the race.

But Kerry lasted a mere six laps that day before hitting the wall and wrecking the car in his Winston Cup debut. His dad finished sixth; his brother was 31st. Kerry,

who started fifth, was 43rd, with five complete laps. Still, he won $21,830.

In October at Lowe's Motor Speedway, the family tried again for a three-Earnhardt race, but Kerry spun out and hit the wall in the fourth turn in a Thursday practice session.

He had planned to run the ARCA race a few days earlier instead, but Dale Sr. and Dave Marcis Racing had worked a deal to put Kerry in a Chevrolet owned by Marcis and set up by Earnhardt Inc.

Marcis tried to qualify the backup car himself but didn't make the field either.

"It was a brand new car, and I never got to test it, never had it on the track before," Kerry Earnhardt said, "and I just got loose and hit the wall. I guess I was just trying to do too much too soon."

Kerry is best known for his success in the ARCA division, where in 2000 and 2001, he had four victories, seven top five finishes and eight top 10s in 11 starts.

TRIBUTES

THE EARLY YEARS

A Few Words for Some of the Best

When NASCAR was getting its start, back in the days of whiskey running and dirt tracks and Saturday night bumper cars, some drivers took their skills to a level that made them well known throughout the South.

In the era before pavement, on into the creation of the first superspeedway, these guys are still remembered decades later for what they accomplished on the track and sometimes away from it.

Here's a look at four of the sport's best from the early days, drivers whose deaths came too soon and whose names are mentioned whenever the conversation turns to the best there ever was.

TINY LUND
(1929-1975)

Valentine's Day 1963 was a big day for Tiny Lund. He was in Daytona, watching a driver named Marvin Panch drive a Maserati experimental car in a practice session around Daytona International Speedway, when the car flew into the air, landed on its roof, slid and caught fire.

Lund was the first to reach Panch and pulled him out of the car. Panch was scheduled to run the Daytona 500, but his injuries would keep him out, so he suggested to the Wood Brothers team that Lund be allowed to drive their Ford in the big race instead.

Lund won. He later was awarded the Carnegie Medal for Heroism.

Lund was born DeWayne Louis Lund in Harlan, Iowa. He started racing motorcycles when he was 15,

then moved on to sprints and midgets but stopped because of his size—he was too big. He settled with modifieds for a while before serving in the air force, then returned to racing in 1955.

In his career, Lund won more than 500 major features and was a four-time NASCAR Grand American division champion—in 1965, 1970, 1971 and 1974.

On August 10, 1975, Lund was fatally injured in a wreck during the Talladega 500.

In 1994, Lund was inducted into the International Motorsports Hall of Fame in Talladega, Alabama.

FIREBALL ROBERTS (1931-1964)

Fireball Roberts didn't get his name from auto racing, though his swiftness around a racetrack would have justified it. He got it for his ability to throw a baseball, a sport he was good at but that didn't hold his interest.

Born Edward Glenn Roberts Jr. in Daytona Beach, he had the type of racing career that leaves people wondering how far it could have taken him. Roberts started racing the Daytona beach course on the sand at age 17, running modifieds, and split his time between modifieds and Winston Cup for five years before going full-time Winston Cup.

Glenn "Fireball" Roberts

He went to the University of Florida, but he never graduated—racing kept getting in the way. Roberts won five races and four poles in 1956 to finish sixth in the point standings. He eventually would win 32 races in 204 starts and set more than 400 track records in his career, including one for most laps led at Darlington, with 1,644. In 1957, he was voted the Winston Cup Series' Most Popular Driver.

It was superspeedways, such as Darlington, that Roberts liked most. He won the 1959 Firecracker 250 at Daytona, and in 1962 he won the Daytona 500 and the Firecracker, becoming the first to win both races at the track in a single season.

But Darlington was his favorite, and he won the Rebel 300 there in 1957 and 1959 and the Southern 500 in 1958 and 1963, when he set a qualifying record of 133.819 mph.

The following year, at Charlotte Motor Speedway, Roberts suffered severe burns when he was involved in a crash with Ned Jarrett and Junior Johnson. He hung on for 37 days before dying of pneumonia, leaving the racing world to wonder just how dominant he would have become.

Fireball Roberts was inducted into the International Motorsports Hall of Fame in 1990.

CURTIS TURNER
(1924-1970)

Curtis Turner lived the lifestyle that got NASCAR started, although there isn't any proof he actually ran moonshine through the hills in the trunk of a souped-up car, since his name isn't found on any police records. But Turner, who was born in Floyd, Virginia, and made a little money in the lumber business, became part of the legend anyway.

One story has him lining up eight full bottles of whiskey in two rows on a highway, the rows making a path barely wider than his Cadillac, then spinning the Caddy 180 degrees and sliding backward between the bottles without touching them.

Herb Thomas, Glen Roberts and Curtis Turner

Turner's first real race was in 1946 in Mount Airy, North Carolina, and he finished last in the 18-car field. He won the second race and became a force in his Oldsmobile through the 1954 season, when he switched to Fords.

In 1950, he led the league in laps completed (1,626), laps led (1,110) and races led (12).

In 1956, he won 22 races in the former convertible division and 17 races, including the Southern 500, in the Grand National class. But he was just as well known for hot-dogging, such as in the Rebel 300 at Darlington when he and Fred Lorenzen ran the last lap fender to fender, with Lorenzen getting in the last bang to win the race. On the "cool down" lap, Turner smashed into Lorenzen, splintering his own car to pieces. He had to walk back to the pits.

Turner's business side from his lumber days helped him later in that he, along with Bruton Smith, got the idea to build a racetrack in 1960 in the Piedmont of North Carolina, and they developed Charlotte Motor Speedway.

His other big business deal had him trying to organize drivers as a local of the Teamsters Union, which didn't sit well with NASCAR president Bill France Sr. and got Turner banned from NASCAR for life. But in 1965, France changed his mind and let Turner back in.

Turner took to racing again and won the American 500 at North Carolina Motor Speed-

way in Rockingham ahead of Cale Yarborough despite driving with a broken rib. He won a few more races, then slipped into retirement, coming back when the race suited him. He was to run the National 500 at Charlotte in 1970, but he was killed in a plane crash at Punxsutawney, Pennsylvania, on October 4 that year.

In 1971, Turner was inducted in the National Motor Sports Press Association's Hall of Fame in Darlington, South Carolina, and in 1992, he was made a member of the International Motorsports Hall of Fame.

JOE WEATHERLY
(1922-1964)

Joseph Herbert Weatherly's training wheels in the sport of racing were attached to a motorcycle. He took an interest in motorcycles while in high school, and when he got out of the army after World War II, the Norfolk, Vir-

ginia, native started racing them and won three American Motorcycle Association Championships.

That done, he switched to stock cars and won 52 modified races and the 1953 NASCAR Modified National Crown. Early in their careers, Weatherly, Fireball Roberts and Curtis Turner all drove for the popular Holman-Moody team. Weatherly and Roberts became friends off the track and reportedly would team up to knock competitors around during races.

Weatherly was voted Most Popular Driver in 1962 and won back-to-back NASCAR Grand National (now Winston Cup) Division Championships in 1962 and 1963, the 1962 title being the first for car owner Bud Moore, whose car he drove to nine victories. The 1963 title came after winning only three races, compared to 14 victories for runner-up Richard Petty, but Weatherly also came through with 35 top 10 finishes in 53 starts.

The stock car racing museum in Darlington, South Carolina, is named for Weatherly, and he was inducted into the International Motorsports Hall of Fame in 1994.

Weatherly was fatally injured in 1964, in a race at Riverside, California. He qualified 16th at the track where, two months earlier, he had clinched his 1963 title. Accounts of his accident differ, but one is that the

transmission in his 1964 red and black No. 8 Mercury malfunctioned, and he pulled into the pits, where Moore's team swapped out the clutch and transmission and sent him back into the race. One theory mentions a stuck accelerator; another blames a brake pin having fallen out. Less than halfway through the race, his car sped into Turn 6 and hit the steel retaining wall, killing him instantly.

His death was reported in the New York Times, alongside a photo of him wearing his "Rebel 300" T-shirt, which he got after winning that race in 1960 at Darlington.

Joe Weatherly

TOO YOUNG, TOO SOON

Sport's Cruel Side Snatches Some Victims

Racing has lost several drivers in recent years—Winston Cup stars, Grand National drivers and some from the Craftsman Truck Series. These are a few whose names still come up in conversation, when someone says "Remember when…" and talks about the great things that could have been.

J. D. McDUFFIE
(1933-1991)

John Delphus McDuffie Jr. never won a race and only had one pole, at Dover in 1978, but he had 653 Winston Cup starts, 12 top five finishes and 106 finishes in the top 10.

But McDuffie, an independent owner-driver, was special to those who followed his career in the No. 70 car. He spent 25 years in Winston Cup, starting in 1966 when it was still called the Grand National circuit. He was a low-budget guy, often working on his car himself and relying on pick-up crews at different tracks to help him move his equipment.

McDuffie was killed in 1991 in a crash during the Global Crossing @ The Glen at Watkins Glen, New York, when his car hit the wall and flipped. He was 52.

McDuffie's dedication to the sport was honored even after his death, when it was assured he would go out the way he would have wanted: He was buried in his racing suit, a cigar between his fingers.

At his funeral, the minister said of McDuffie's passion for the sport, "If you cut him, he'd bleed Havoline."

Opposite: Rob Moroso and Mark Martin

ROB MOROSO
(1968 –1990)

Rob Moroso was supposed to be a young star, just beginning his ascent into NASCAR's elite. But one night near Mooresville, North Carolina, after a race that day at North Wilkesboro, he was going too fast—75 mph in a 35 mph zone—and didn't make the curve in the road. The accident killed him and his female passenger.

Moroso was the defending Busch Series champion and in contention for 1990 Winston Cup rookie of the year. But his off-track record wasn't as good and it was found that he had several speeding tickets on file and had been allowed to keep his driver's license because local courts had given him a break.

In one of his last races, the Goody's 500 at Martinsville in September, 1990, Moroso started 28th and finished 21st in his Crown Oldsmobile. He died on September 30.

JOHN NEMECHEK
(1970–1997)

John Nemechek's death, after a race at Homestead in 1997, made him the first-ever truck race fatality.

In November, 1997, Winston Cup driver Joe Nemechek, John's brother, raced at Homestead in the Jiffy Lube 300 and led 127 of 200 laps to win the race.

In an emotional interview afterward, Joe said, "I lost my brother, who was also my best friend, in Turn 1 ear-lier this year. To come back and win the race, I don't even know what to say. It's unbelievable. I know this one was for him."

John's accident came in the Florida Dodge Dealers 400 on March 21, when his truck hit the wall in Turn 1. He sustained massive brain injuries and died five days later. John, a native of Lakeland, Florida, was 27.

TONY ROPER
(1964 –2000)

Only two people have died in truck races, John Nemechek and Tony Roper.

Roper became the first fatality at Texas Motor Speedway, which opened in 1997, when his truck was involved in a fiery crash during the O'Reilly 400. He was pulled from the wreck and taken to a hospital, where a trauma surgeon said a neck injury kept blood from flowing to Roper's brain. He was unconscious but put on a ventilator. His dad, former short track driver Dean Roper, was with him when he died, a few hours later.

Roper was born in Springfield, Missouri but lived in Concord, North Carolina with his wife, Michelle. He had made 60 career Truck Series starts, the best year coming in 1998 when he started 27 races and had one top five finish and six top 10s.

Roper also raced the Busch series for two years and in 1999 had three top 10s in 19 races. He started his career driving late models in 1986, then moved to the ASA stock circuit in 1992. His first truck run was in 1995.

On the fatal night in Texas, October 14, he had tried to move through traffic, but bumped another truck then veered sharply to the right and hit the wall along the frontstretch head-on, causing his truck to explode in flames.

Tony Roper was 35. Somehow, the tragedy made his father feel the need to climb back in a race car, and he did. But 10 months later, on August 19, 2001, during a 100-mile ARCA race at the Illinois State Fair, Dean Roper's car crashed head-on into a wall, and he, too, was killed.

Alan Kulwicki
December 14, 1954 – April 1, 1993

If Alan Kulwicki were to have had a theme song, it could have been "My Way." And his way was not always at the top of the common-sense meter.

When Junior Johnson was so impressed by his talent that he asked Kulwicki to drive his cars, Kulwicki said no. He'd rather be owner/driver of his own team, thank you, and work on the cars himself. Armed with a degree in mechanical engineering from the University of Wisconsin, the Greenfield, Wisconsin native knew how to build cars and make them fly.

He did give in to outside help once, when he got the Hooters restaurant chain to sponsor his No. 7 Ford Thunderbird, giving him the money to compete with the big guys.

Kulwicki's first Winston Cup race was in 1985, and his first full season was in 1986, when he was Rookie of the Year. In 1988, at Phoenix, he found out what it was like to win.

In 1992, Kulwicki got his way in the best manner possible. Defending Winston Cup champion Dale Earnhardt was trying to join Cale Yarborough as the only other driver to win three consecutive titles. Bill Elliott, who said yes to Junior Johnson, also was in the hunt.

And Davey Allison was ready to win his first Cup trophy.

But Kulwicki didn't see it like that. In the last race of the season, at Atlanta Motor Speedway, the scenario played out like a movie script. Richard Petty was running his last race. Jeff Gordon was running his first. Allison, Elliott and Kulwicki entered the race each with a shot at the points title.

Elliott won the race, but Kulwicki won the Winston Cup Championship by 10 points because he led the most laps.

In his entire career, Kulwicki only won five races in 207 starts, but he had 38 top fives, 75 top 10s and 24 poles.

On April 1, 1993, he was in a private aircraft headed for the race at Bristol, when the plane went down. He was 38.

Even after his death, Kulwicki has people doing things his way. When he would win, Kulwicki would drive his car clockwise around the track for his encore, the Polish Victory Lap.

Still, to this day, other drivers do the same, in honor of his memory.

Davey Allison's death shocked the racing community, because when a driver is hurt or killed, it's simply not supposed to happen this way.

Allison was part of the racing fraternity known as The Alabama Gang, a group of car runners headquartered in the Birmingham suburb of Hueytown, Alabama,

that included the Allison brothers Bobby and Donnie and their families, the Bonnett family, racer Red Farmer, and, by marriage, driver Hut Strickland.

Davey and Clifford Allison were Bobby's sons, and Strickland married their sister Pam.

Like pieces coming loose from a puzzle, the racing Alabama Gang slowly fell apart until now, only Strickland and Farmer remain.

Davey Allison was piloting his new helicopter when it went down in a field at Talladega Superspeedway.

Clifford Allison died 11 months before Davey, in a practice session at Michigan. Neil Bonnett died seven months after Davey, in a practice run at Daytona. Five years earlier, Bobby gave up racing after a severe accident at Pocono.

Farmer, a casual short track driver, was with Davey as a passenger in the helicopter on July 12, 1993, when they decided to cruise up from Hueytown to Talladega to watch David Bonnett, Neil's son, test a car. The helicopter crashed in the speedway's infield. Farmer was injured. Davey Allison died the next day of head injuries.

Fans and drivers reacted.

T-shirts were seen that said, "Davey's gone one lap ahead."

On July 18, after Dale Earnhardt won the series' next race, at Pocono, he circled the track with a No. 28 flag flying from the window of his Chevrolet.

One fan ordered a license plate that read 28 MIS U.

Davey Allison had his moments of fame, among them the 1988 Daytona 500, when he finished second to his dad. A newspaper columnist asked Bobby's wife and Davey's mother, Judy, if she was cheering for her husband or her son. "I was for Bobby," she said. "He pays the bills."

Davey Allison was survived by his wife, Liz, and their children, Krista and Robbie, his parents Bobby and Judy, his sisters Bonnie and Carrie and Pam, his grandmother Kitty Allison, Clifford's wife Elisa, and their children Brandon, Tanya and Leslie.

Davey and Liz Allison had been married a mere five years. They had designed their dream home and lived in it only six months.

Davey Allison was 32. It's simply not supposed to happen this way.

Neil Bonnett
July 30, 1946 – February 11, 1994

Neil Bonnett had raced, he had won, he had skipped around the South with the hard-charging Alabama Gang, with the Allisons and Red Farmer and the rest.

He started off racing short tracks near his hometown of Hueytown, Alabama, and won a few of the big shows, including the 1980 Talladega 500 and the Southern 500 in 1981.

It was at Darlington, in 1990, that Bonnett had an accident that put his racing on hold and sent him into a long period of rehabilitation.

And so, with the source of his livelihood from 1974 to 1990 stored away, he did some television, hosting *Neil Bonnett's Winners* on The Nashville Network.

But something about driving a fast car stayed with Bonnett, and at age 47, in 1994, he got back in a stock car. He received medical clearance on July 25, 1993, and resumed his career at Talladega.

Bonnett died in a single-car crash during a practice session for the 1994 Daytona 500. He was survived by his wife, Susan, and children David and Kristen.

In almost 18 years on the Winston Cup tour, Bonnett had 18 victories, including back-to-back wins in the longest race—the 1982 and 1983 Coca-Cola 600s. He also won back-to-back Busch Clashes (now called the Bud Shootout) at Daytona in 1983 and 1984.

In 1985, he was fourth in the points race—the year his teammate, Darrell Waltrip, won the championship. In all, he had 362 Winston Cup starts, 83 top five finishes and 20 poles.

In 1997, Neil Bonnett won one more honor: He was inducted into the National Motorsports Press Association's Hall of Fame.

Adam Petty
July 10, 1980 – May 12, 2000

Sometimes, the cruel side of auto racing rises up and snatches another victim, compressing the whole entity of NASCAR—drivers, crews, fans—into a joint state of mourning.

It was a practice session, not a race, when Adam Petty crashed. He was running at New Hampshire International Speedway, a 1.058-mile oval in Loudon, New Hampshire. His family wasn't there for this trip. His mother and brother were home at the family's farm in North Carolina. His father and sister were en route to England, where Montgomery Lee was to participate in an equestrian event.

Adam Petty was 19.

At about 12:15 p.m., during Friday practice for Saturday's Busch 200 Grand National race, Petty's No. 45 Chevrolet spun and hit the Turn 3 wall head on at an estimated 130 miles per hour. He was cut from the car and taken by ambulance to a helicopter pad outside the track, then airlifted to Concord Hospital.

He was pronounced dead there at about 12:45 p.m. A hospital spokesperson gave the cause as head trauma. A stuck throttle was suspected to have caused the accident.

Petty was the first fourth-generation driver to compete in NASCAR's Winston Cup series, officially getting that title on April 11, 1998, when he made his professional racing debut at Peach State Speedway in Jefferson, Georgia.

At the time of his crash, the son of Kyle and Pattie Huffman Petty, the grandson of Richard and Lynda and great-grandson of Lee, was one of three teenagers driving the circuit. The others were 19-year-olds Casey Atwood and Justin Labonte.

The cruel side of auto racing was not new to the Petty family on that day in May 2000. On April 5, 2000, Lee Petty had died at age 86 of complications from stomach surgery.

Adam Petty accomplished much in his 19 years

When he was 16, his father let him drive around the track at Darlington, South Carolina, in a street car. "I knew right then what he was going to do," Kyle Petty said.

In September 1998, at age 18 years, three months, Adam became the youngest Automobile Racing Club of America (ARCA) winner in history, replacing his dad, who won at 18 years, eight months, when he won at Lowe's Motor Speedway near Charlotte, North Carolina.

Adam Petty's father and grandfather joined him that day in Victory Lane.

"I'm honored to be a Petty," he once said. "My dad and grandfather put no pressure on me at all. I just do the best I can."

Adam also was the youngest to ever win an American Speed Association (ASA) series event. He was in his second full season on the Grand National circuit and planned to run full-time Winston Cup in 2001.

He did make one Winston Cup start, on April 2, 2000, at Texas. His father didn't make the field. Adam's engine failed on Lap 216. On Lap 228, Kyle came in, in relief of driver Elliott Sadler, driving Sadler's No. 21 Ford.

But father and son never were on the track at the same time in a Winston Cup race.

Adam Petty's memorial service, billed as a celebration rather than a funeral, was held on Monday, May 15, 2000 at the Mills Center at High Point University in High Point, North Carolina.

The 50-minute service was in a basketball gymnasium, with a simple platform and podium at the front. Longtime family friend Rev. Doug Carty led the service.

Adam's 14-year-old sister Montgomery Lee was the only family member to speak. Adam's 18-year-old brother, Austin, gave Rev. Carty a note from which to read.

Among Montgomery Lee's statements: "He won't be there for the birth of my first child, whose name will have 'Adam' somewhere in it." She said that, on the Wednesday before his death, Adam let her cut his hair—a demonstration of trust. "Adam loved everyone and treated everyone equally. And because of that, everyone fell in love with him."

From Austin's note: Memories of Adam at age six, asking his grandmother to sponsor his go-kart. And Austin, who resembles Adam, taping a note to the back of his hat while at a racetrack. The note read: "I'm not Adam, so don't ask for my autograph."

Faces in the crowd at the memorial included car owners Rick Hendrick, Robert Yates, Bill Davis, Felix Sabates and drivers Jeff and Ward Burton, John Andretti, Dale Jarrett, Bobby Labonte, Bill Elliott, Sterling Marlin, Johnny Benson, Joe Nemechek and Geoffrey Bodine. Also there were NASCAR president Bill France Jr., chief operating officer Mike Helton, Lowe's Motor Speedway president H. A. "Humpy" Wheeler, and former drivers Ernie Irvan, Ned Jarrett, Benny Parsons and Bobby Allison.

An estimated 1,000 attended.

Close friends followed afterward to Kyle and Pattie Petty's farm in Trinity, N.C.

That part of the day, honoring the first fourth-generation driver, will always be private.

No cameras were allowed.

Kenny Irwin
August 5, 1969 – July 7, 2000

It was spooky, the way racing took the life of Kenny Irwin.

Eight weeks to the day after Adam Petty died, Irwin's blue Chevrolet wrecked on almost the same spot, on the same track, in a practice session—just like Petty.

Irwin was practicing for the New England 300 at New Hampshire International Speedway when his car struck the wall entering Turn 3 and flipped onto its roof. He had hit the wall at an estimated 150 miles per hour. The cause of death, a spokesperson for nearby Concord Hospital said, was "multiple injuries."

As with Adam Petty's accident, initial thought was that Irwin's car had a stuck accelerator. Petty's problem was blamed on a stuck throttle, also.

It was spooky in that Irwin once drove the No. 28 Ford, which Davey Allison drove and which Ernie Irvan almost lost his life in when he crashed at Michigan in 1994.

When word of Irwin's death was heard, drivers found a place to put the blame.

Mark Martin criticized the layout of the track. "This racetrack and Martinsville are a particular danger to stuck throttles because the corners are so sharp," he said.

Rusty Wallace said there was a bump in the track, at the end of the backstretch.

Ward Burton said the almost-flat turns needed to be banked higher.

"These are the days that make you really sit back and look at yourself in the mirror and ask, 'Why do I do this?'" Wallace said.

In addition to stock cars, Irwin drove the truck circuit and was Craftsman Truck Series Rookie of the Year in 1997. He had three poles and four top five finishes in his car but was winless in 87 starts. He was Winston Cup Rookie of the Year in 1998.

At age six, he started competing in midget cars, roaring around at 40 miles per hour. He was 1996 National Midget Series Champion.

Irwin is survived by his mother Reva, father Kenny Sr., and three sisters.

Dale Earnhardt
April 29, 1951 – February 18, 2001

Perhaps the saddest words ever spoken in the history of NASCAR were those by president Mike Helton, as he addressed the media gathered at Halifax Medical Center in Daytona Beach, Florida, at 7 p.m. on February 18, 2001.

In a speech televised to millions, Helton said, "This is undoubtedly one of the most difficult announcements I've ever had to make, but after the accident in Turn 4 at the end of the Daytona 500, we've lost Dale Earnhardt."

Earnhardt was magic. Love him or hate him, everyone knew who he was on a racetrack. Everyone watched to see what this Houdini of a driver would do next, who he'd "accidently" brush aside to create an opening. When he died, other drivers' fans mourned as much as the No. 3 faithful: Now that the master was gone, who would their guy race against?

What was the point of competition?

When he died, on the last lap of the Daytona 500, he did it protecting the lead of his son, Dale Jr., and teammate Michael Waltrip, the eventual winner. He was running third, keeping the traffic away, when his car slammed the outside concrete wall of the 2.5-mile Daytona International Speedway after making contact with the car of Sterling Marlin, then being hit in the side by the car of Ken Schrader.

His black Chevrolet slid backward across the track and came to rest in the grass, about 300 yards from the start-finish line.

Emergency workers rushed in. He was cut from the car and airlifted to the hospital. He was pronounced dead at 5:16 p.m.

Dale Earnhardt was born in Kannapolis, North Carolina, the son of Ralph and Martha Earnhardt, the third of their five children. His daddy was a dirt track driver, one of the best in his day, with a 23-year racing career and more than 500 recorded victories. Ralph would work on his cars in the garage, out back behind the family's home on Sedan Avenue in Kannapolis, as young Dale watched and played with toy cars on the floor.

Ralph Earnhardt died of a heart attack while working in that garage, on September 26, 1973, at age 45.

By then, Dale, 22, already knew what he wanted to be when he grew up. He ran some Grand National races, was Winston Cup Rookie of the Year in 1979 and won the Winston Cup Championship in 1980, his first of seven, tying Richard Petty for the most ever.

He got the attention of the older, more established drivers, with his get-out-of-my-way style and fierce attitude in the car, which earned him the nickname The Intimidator.

He won the Winston Cup title again in 1986, 1987, 1990, 1991, 1993 and 1994 and brought in more than $40 million to go with his 76 Winston Cup victories. In 1987, he even won six of the first eight races on the schedule.

But the one race that mattered most to him took him 20 tries to win.

The Daytona 500, the opening act of the show every season, eluded Earnhardt until 1998, when he ended a 59-race winless drought with the biggest celebration of his life. After stopping for right-side tires and fuel with 30 laps to go, Earnhardt stayed in the front until the caution flag flew on Lap 199 following a collision between Jimmy Spencer and John Andretti.

"It was my time. I don't care how we won it, but we won it," he said later.

The postrace response was incredible. Crew members, hundreds of them, from every stop along pit road, jumped the wall to touch Earnhardt's hand as his car

inched by. He pulled his Chevrolet into the infield grass and spun doughnuts until a "3" was carved in the turf. Fans rushed from the grandstands to grab a clump of grass and handful of dirt and save it for eternity.

"I cried a little bit in the race car on the way to the checkered flag," he said later. "Well, maybe not cried, but at least my eyes watered up."

Dale Earnhardt was 17 when he married Latane Key, and the two had a son, Kerry. He divorced at 19 and later married Brenda Gee, daughter of car builder Robert Gee, for whom Earnhardt once worked. They had two children, Kelley and Dale Jr.

But that marriage, too, dissolved, and in 1982 Earnhardt married Teresa Houston, daughter of racer Hal Houston. They had a daughter, Taylor Nicole.

His mother, Martha, still lives in the little white house on Sedan Avenue in Kannapolis, where the Earnhardts are able to be just local folks despite Dale's worldwide celebrity.

When he died, the people of Kannapolis, of all of Cabarrus County, of all of the country, reacted. Flowers were piled high at the gate to Dale and Teresa's home in nearby Mooresville and outside the adjacent race shop. Fans drove a thousand miles to pay their respects.

It was like losing Elvis, one fan said, or Princess Diana—someone who just wasn't supposed to go yet.

Dale Earnhardt was buried on Wednesday, February 21, 2001, at an undisclosed location following a private family service. The next day, an invitation-only memorial service was held at Calvary Church in Charlotte, the largest church in

the area. It was televised. Out of respect, the fans who came to that followed the family's wishes and stayed back, content to be a part of it but not in the way.

Singer Randy Owen of the group Alabama sang two songs, and Dale Beaver, a chaplain with Motor Racing Outreach, spoke of Earnhardt as a caring, loving father, who wanted to make his family, friends and those around him happy.

Away from the racetrack, Dale Earnhardt was a regular guy—quiet, calm and exceedingly polite, a family man, a country kid from Kannapolis who just happened to be one of the most recognized faces in the world.

On the track, he was the pilot of a wild, motorized black stallion that went wherever he steered it, no matter what was in the way. Like magic.

"Everybody thought he would grow old," his sister Kaye said.

Dale Earnhardt was 49.

NEW GENERATIONS

DALE EARNHARDT, JR.
Born November 10, 1974

Ralph Dale Earnhardt Junior may have the same name as one of NASCAR's most famous drivers of all time, but Little E is different from his dad in many ways. He's been known to speed around in a Corvette, play drums onstage with rock 'n' roll bands and buddy up to millionaire athletes and movie stars. He has a gathering place in his basement known as "Club E," where friends meet to party until all hours. He likes his music loud.

But on the racetrack, Dale Jr. shows a lot of his upbringing.

Earnhardt Jr. graduated from Mooresville (North Carolina) High School in 1992 and attended a trade school for two years. He and his half-brother Kerry found a 1978 Monte Carlo in a junkyard, fixed it up and started racing at Concord Motorsport Park. Earnhardt Jr. made his Grand National debut on June 22, 1996 at Myrtle Beach Speedway in South Carolina, in the Carolina Pride 250. He qualified seventh, lost a lap in the pits and finished 14th. He won $1,880.

He had one top 10 finish that year, a seventh place in the Detroit Gasket 200 at Michigan International Speedway in August.

Then in 1998, he ran his first full season on the Grand National circuit, won seven races and became the Busch Series champion. For that, he credited his father and said, "I guess it will sink in once I see the look in Daddy's eyes."

He did so well that in September that year he received a six-year sponsorship from Budweiser, even though he had never driven a Winston Cup car. He did run a few Winston Cup races in 1999, the first being the Coca-Cola 600 in May at Lowe's Motor Speedway, which

was met with a huge media build-up. When it was over, Earnhardt was 16th, 10 places behind his dad.

Earnhardt Jr. won his second Grand National title in 1999, then moved full-time to Winston Cup in 2000, where he won three races—at Texas, Richmond and Charlotte—and made NASCAR history in that father and son each raced a full season together.

When Dale Earnhardt died on February 18, 2001, in Daytona, Dale Jr. was faced with the enormous challenge of growing up and carrying on what his dad had tried to teach him. "I had this little bit of brat in me," he said a few weeks later. "That's all gone now."

He showed his true ability when NASCAR returned to Daytona on July 7, 2001, for the Pepsi 400.

He won.

TONY STEWART
Born May 20, 1971

Tony Stewart jumped into NASCAR Winston Cup racing in 1999 after competing in open-wheel Indy cars. The transition was easy for him, which he proved in qualifying for the season-opening Daytona 500—he had a lap of 194.599 and started on the front row next to Jeff Gordon.

He won his first pole later that season at Martinsville and won his first of three races at Richmond.

"None of us dreamed he'd win a race," said his car owner, Joe Gibbs. "We thought he'd be up close. None of us dreamed he'd be in the top 10 [in points], much less the top five."

Stewart finished his first season as Rookie of the Year and fourth in the points race.

He started racing at age eight and won the International Karting Foundation Grand National Championship in 1983, the World Karting Association national championship in 1987, and was U.S. Auto Club sprint car Rookie of the Year in 1991. In 1995, he won the USAC triple crown, with national titles in midgets, sprint cars and the Silver Crown series.

But his interest was in open-wheel racing, and in 1996 he started the Indianapolis 500 from the pole, led

43 laps and was named the race's top rookie. That year, Stewart met Joe Gibbs and took an interest in stock cars. While winning the Indy Racing League championship in 1997, Stewart also drove five races for Gibbs's NASCAR team. He drove 22 races for him in 1998 and won two poles and finished second twice.

In 1999, the lure to do both Indy Car and Winston Cup in one day was irresistible. On May 30, Stewart raced the Indy 500, finishing ninth. He flew to Charlotte and also competed in the Coca-Cola 600, where he started last for missing the driver's meeting. He finished fourth, completing 1,100 miles in one day.

After Stewart's first Winston Cup victory, in 1999 at Richmond, he said, "It's unbelievable. To do it in my rookie season, I think it's going to hit even harder tomorrow morning."

Said Jeff Gordon, "Tony Stewart is a great talent, and Joe Gibbs's guys have put a great car under him."

Tony Stewart was born in Columbus, Indiana. His race shop in is Huntersville, North Carolina. His dream, he says, is to one day win the Indianapolis 500.

KEVIN HARVICK
Born December 8, 1975

It's interesting that Kevin Harvick's first Winston Cup ride was with Richard Childress Racing.

When Dale Earnhardt was a toddler, he watched his dad work on race cars in their backyard garage while he played with toy cars on the floor.

When Harvick was a baby, he watched from his playpen as his dad worked on race cars in their garage.

When he "graduated" from kindergarten in 1980, Harvick's parents gave him a go-kart, and in 10 years behind the wheels of the little speedsters, Harvick won seven National Championships and two Grand National Championships.

Harvick was a Busch Series driver when tragedy—Earnhardt's death in the 2001 Daytona 500—put him in a Winston Cup car, taking on the No. 29 Goodwrench Chevrolet for Richard Childress Racing.

He was the Busch Series Rookie of the Year in 2000. He won three races and finished third in points, and in 2001, he won in only his third Winston Cup start at Atlanta while continuing a Busch schedule that led to his winning that circuit's championship on the strength of five victories and 20 top five finishes.

He became the first driver to run full-time in both the Busch and Winston Cup series in the same season—a work detail of 69 races.

Harvick had briefly attended Bakersfield Junior College in his hometown of Bakersfield, Calif., after high school to study architecture, but he changed his mind.

"The time came for me to make a choice about my future," he said. "I chose racing, and I've never looked back."

Another decision about his future came on February 28, 2001, when Harvick married DeLana Linville in a ceremony in Las Vegas.

Harvick's winning the Busch title in 2001 made Childress the first car owner to win a championship in each major NASCAR series—Winston Cup, Busch and Craftsman Truck.

MATT KENSETH
Born March 10, 1972

Matt Kenseth, a native of Cambridge, Wisc., who lives in Terrel, N.C., started his racing career in high school when he started running stock cars in 1988 at age 16. It didn't take long for him to figure out what to do—the high school junior won his first feature race in only his third start.

His interest in the sport actually began a few years earlier, when at age 13 his dad bought him a race car and said he'd race it himself if Kenseth would help work on the car. When Kenseth turned 16, the car would be his.

At age 19, Kenseth was racing late models on Wisconsin tracks and became the youngest winner every in the ARTGO Challenge Series, breaking the record set by current Rousch Racing teammate Mark Martin.

In 1994, Kenseth won track titles at two Wisconsin venues, and in 1995 he won 15 of a possible 60 races, making him the state's late-model champion.

In 1997, Kenseth got a phone call from Robbie Reiser of Reiser Enterprises, and he packed up and moved to the Busch Series, where he was second in points in his first full season and had three wins and 17 top fives.

The year 2000 was special in that Kenseth became the first rookie to win the Coca-Cola 600 at Lowe's Motor Speedway, near Charlotte, North Carolina.

He did it in just his 18th Winston Cup start.

JIMMIE JOHNSON
Born September 17, 1975

Jimmie Johnson was born in El Cajon, California and wasn't even old enough for kindergarten when he got his career rolling—literally.

Johnson started riding motorcycles at age four, then switched to four wheels and raced trucks when he was old enough to drive them

His efforts soon turned to cars, and in 1998 he ran three Busch Series races and was named ASA rookie of the year after finishing fourth in the division's point standings in his first full season.

He ran five Busch races in 1999, and in 2000 he finished 10th in points and third in the battle for Rookie of the Year. In 2001, Johnson figured he was ready for Winston Cup, and in October, he qualified 15th and finished 39th in his first start, the UAW-GM Quality 500 at Lowe's Motor Speedway near his current residence of Mooresville, North Carolina.

He opened 2002 with a memorable career highlight—winning the pole for the Daytona 500.

Johnson drives the No. 48 Lowe's car for Hendrick Motorsports.

MBNA PLATINUM 400
DOVER INTERNATIONAL SPEEDWAY
WINNER • JUNE 2, 2002

RYAN NEWMAN
Born December 8, 1977

Ryan Newman was born in South Bend, Indiana, began racing quarter-midgets at age four and immediately started padding his resume with championships by taking Rookie of the Year awards in the midgets, Silver Crown and sprint car series.

Newman won the national Silver Crown title in 1999. When he first strapped himself into a stock car, he was ready to show his stuff—he won the second race he ever entered, an ARCA event at Pocono in 2000.

Newman hooked up with Roger Penske for his big rides and won the pole for the Coca Cola 600 in 2000 in just his third Winston Cup start.

Of course, he had studied up on how to do it—Newman has a degree from Purdue University, where he studied interdisciplinary engineering.

His specialty was vehicle dynamics.

KURT BUSCH
Born August 4, 1978

Kurt Busch began to show off his talent at an early age, in a city where showing off is quite welcome.

He started his career racing dwarf cars in 1994 at Pahrump Valley Speedway, a quarter-mile clay track near his hometown, Las Vegas. By 1996, he was steering Legends cars and was Rookie of the Year, and he was Rookie of the Year in 2000 when he drove the NASCAR Truck series for Roush Racing.

When Roush signed him, Busch decided to play it safe. He didn't quit his day job, fixing water mains with the Las Vegas Valley Water District—instead, he asked for a one-year leave of absence, just in case this racing thing didn't work out.

Busch, who says his favorite subject in school was math, soon calculated that fixing water mains wasn't going to be his career choice. He kept racing and soon had enough money to spend on himself. Someone asked him what gift he would buy for his own use. His choice: A PlayStation 2.

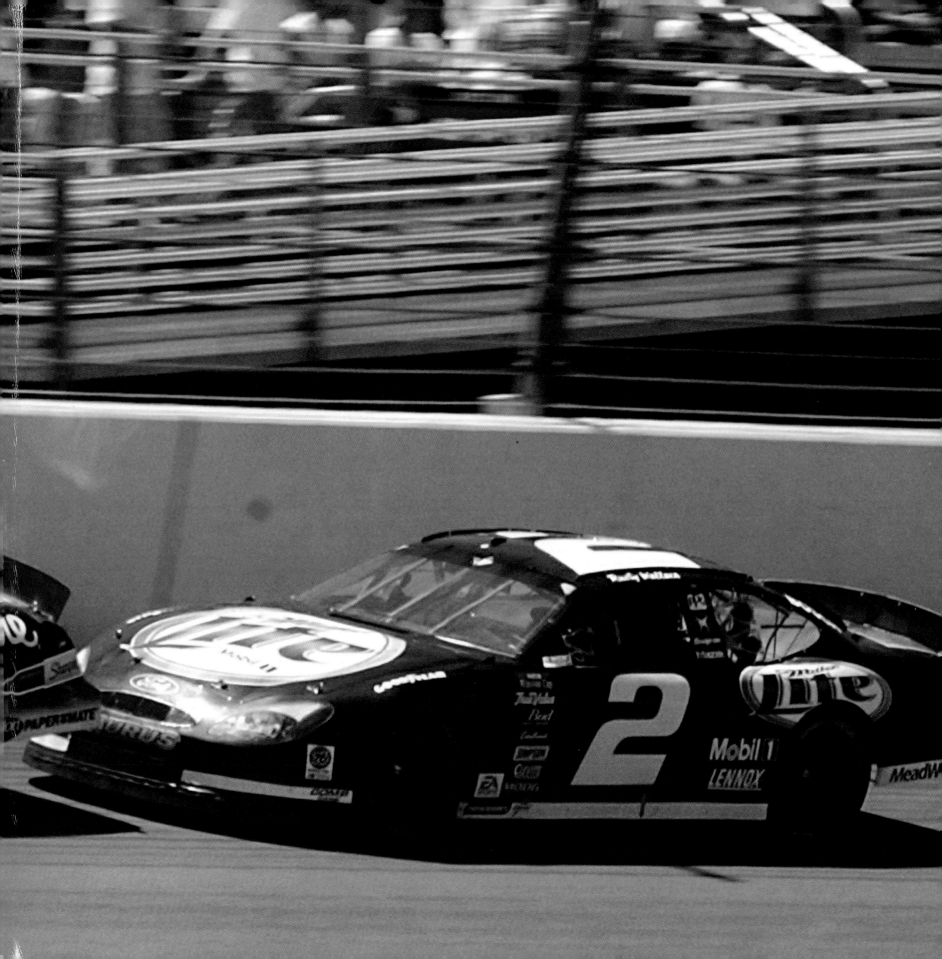

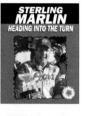

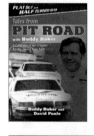